THE MIRROR of Actuality

ELIZABETH JANE PARKER

THE MIRROR OF Actuality

MEMOIRS

Cirencester

Also by Elizabeth Jane Parker

The Theory and Revelation of Angels Cosmos Earth A.C.E.
Grosvenor House, 2009 - ISBN 978-1907211812

Voices from Heaven
AuthorHouse 2011 - ISBN 978-1456771782

Published by Memoirs

MEMOIRS
PUBLISHING

25 Market Place, Cirencester, Gloucestershire, GL7 2NX
info@memoirsbooks.co.uk www.memoirspublishing.com

ISBN: 978-1-909020-44-3

FOR MY MOTHER
EILEEN DOROTHY TYRRELL

TABLE OF CONTENTS

....

SPIRITUAL ASSIGNMENT

....

Knowledge and Connection with Actuality
and Spiritual Assignment

To Elizabeth Jane Parker from dimensions of reality and reasoning

With Heaven 2012

....

The reality and reasoning of *spiritual assignation* is homage to our placement and bearing within life. The actual diversity of life is the procreative vibration of all living things and connection with an *electromotive force* with and without physical formation. From our senses and biology, the miracle and transformation of life and journey enable us all to understand *elementary epigraph and epistemology* upon our planet Earth. The phenomena of actuality and time, together volumetrically with science, converge into belief with electrons of the human brain and all of nature as one electroencephalograph with everyday existence and appreciation. So, from this *sporadic dimension* the whole picture of *God and belief brings* aspects of love, honour and truth to our Planet through a portal of dimension circumnavigating the Globe. So, the reality of life and reasoning within our Universe is ever moving around the Cosmos and the labyrinth of bio creation. Every day there are imperceptive movements and changes to our World. The realism of this exists each day we live within bio chemistry, however, learning from

1

our metaphoric changes we as humanity forget to understand the miracle of our lives and intelligences. The truth is we are all part of an *eternal diameter* with geometrics and mathematical assimilations.

We as humanity have the power, intelligence and understanding to reciprocate the miracle of our lives. We as humanity have the ability to make the changes that are now necessary for our lives and realism with belief in our *God and his Holy Angels.*

The connections and spiritual aspects of communication is one of hierarchical domains of physics and ethereal phosphorous vibration. *The Systematic Synchronic Systems* relating to us all as a world united are yet to be heard by humanity as one whole being. *Heaven and Earth* are the realities of our journey and life itself. The aspect and perceptions are important for our individualism and purpose. However, insular aspects and opinion become a projection of modern theory and a living miracle is simply taken for granted. This is a truth within the *Twenty-First Century.* We as humanity are indeed a wonderful and intellectual species upon our Planet Earth. We have achieved a great intelligence with life and reasoning and sadly from this we have overlooked our basic foundations and realities with our journey through time and space. The fragmentation of religion, politics and disbelief in the wonder of evolution has brought us again into dilemma.

Our planet is consumed with zillions of life cells and photoelectric vibration within a moment in time each day we live. Through eternity and space we all evolved. This truth has taken millions of eons to establish the world we live in today. *This World is the wonder of the Universe.* We all have life and gift within her sphere. We all have the ability to SEE (*Spiritual*

Evolution Event) and understand the time and motion of our journey with hers. The imponderable idyllic hydrographs of vibration and establishment upon Earth for us as humanity is brought through our lives by our sight and transcendence within our biology. Her landscape is one of inspiration and peace to our soul in major. However the truth is we as mankind are currently diminishing her sustainability with materialism and desire. How do we in truth, SEE our *elementary epigraph and epistemology* maintaining our future lives without the beauty and inspiration of our natural world?

Responsibility is something we all need to learn as humanity. The major domino effect is brought by individualism learning, sustaining and appreciating the beauty and eternal transformations of our Mother Earth. The reality of *The New Age* is about transformations and honour among men and women of our World. So simple is this vibration that it has been globally overlooked and insidiously maintaining the dark clusters circulating our planet at present. From this analogy man fails to SEE and absorb the beauty of life and the meaning of connection and reconnection with Heaven.

This book is a teaching book by *Spiritual Assignation* from a directive of purpose and understanding our elementary epigraph and epistemology from *Heaven unto Earth*. The believability of this is by choice. However, teaching and learning is the aspiration of us all with virtue, truth and love. This book will enable disbelievers and sceptics to find some inspiration *about God and his Holy Angels*. The times allotted to us all are of great value within our Universe and evolution. But most of all there is another dimension for which we return upon our demise. The reality of this is not believed by many people of our modern era. However, the journey of life is a wonderful experience for our *Heavenly Bodies*. Each and every day of life we can find peace and understanding through suffering and disappointment. However, to find this we must all overcome our disavowals to the holy covenants which exist through time and generations within the realms of reality and connection with Heaven. Once we believe, truly believe in God and Earth being part of a superstructure and innovation through our lives together, we can be truly enlightened and connected through love, honour and truth.

An Angel Ray taken by Elizabeth Jane Parker and when enlarged you can SEE both a mountain and the roots of a tree. 2011.

Spiritual Path is...

Learning about our Divine Understanding within the confines of mortality, our life expectancy is just a small speck and particle of the magnitude of living. Our presence upon Earth is to manifest our memories of love and light. The enigma and encapsulation of God is the virtuous learning through life seeking and learning about our faith and love of all things. To know that God is personal to us all is the reasoning of our passage with light and our Earth as one. The power of God is with us all through love, honour and truth. The Holy Trinity is with blessings and accumulation of virtue.

Elizabeth Jane Parker 2012.

THE MIRROR OF ACTUALITY

....

By Elizabeth Jane Parker

....

Many people within our world today simply don't believe. The question about belief is exactly *how did this all start*? How did intelligence begin? 'How did?' is the eternal question. From this we understand about theory. We understand about revelation but still we search, still we wonder, still we learn.

Another question about theory is why, where and when did man evolve? We have theory, we have research but as yet metaphorically speaking no *concrete* revelation. What exactly is the secret of life? What is life? What is reason? What is truth?

Again we ask, what is the purpose of life? Where and how did the Universe begin? Theoretically we believe there was a *big bang!* The question here is *do we definitely know this happened*? Scientists experiment and theorise. They believe with research that they have the definitive meaning of our cosmos and theoretical faction with reality. From experimentation they bring theory on a small scale. They bring mathematics and scientific assimilations. However, the truth is, the mystery still remains. Theoretically we are still mystified and are inconclusive about the reality of our beginnings. Our intelligence constantly seeks answers with theoretical analysis. What is intelligence? What is belief? What is knowledge? The introspection and projection of diversity with humanity is that intelligence has many forms and directives with belief and knowledge. Belief is a directive no matter what we have as an opinion. Knowledge is about learning and growth. It is just so with spiritual paths where the definitive meaning of virtue is based upon research. We all search for reasoning during our life.

The truths are the workings of our *Universe* and are eternally changing. Yesterday's theory and yesterday's system are not systematically the same. This is the wonder of intelligence and searching. As we all search with our soul within life Scientists search for fact. However, the questions and answers of life is the eternal truth with transformation. This transformation is the mystery of synthesis and absorption with the evolution of time and space. The mystery becomes the *eternal mystery* with natural elements and direction with our Earth and her journey. The questions and answers with time bring us all to direct and reform our knowledge into betterment and provision for a future sustainability with life and our journey through space. Thus, to clearly understand our journey with wisdom and knowledge is the greater perspective of hope and a future life with God and our soul's journey.

Now we move on into an examination of major reasoning with our astrophysics contained within biological confinement during our life span with the *"White Light of Reasoning"* and our Earth moving around the Sun. We journey with our planet and within our modern age we take for granted the miracle and wonders that life gives to us all from her very essence with science. Our spiritual one is contained biologically within her sphere. Is this fact or truth? However, the reality analysis of God and reasoning is currently one of conjecture with belief among mankind, and the global diversity of *theism and tendentious* opinion becomes one of irreconcilable differences about religion and politics. For many people we understand that God is all loving and compassionate and yet we as mankind are divided throughout the globe.

Our planet Earth is a miracle of life moving around the cosmos and we are but a small grain of sand with ecology and evolution. Our intelligence during our modern age has lost all aspects of the reality of God and *the holy covenants* regarding our journey with Earth. We fail to recognise Earth and her *holy spirit* with nature and life as one. We as humanity have yet to actually *understand and see* this as a reality with life and reasoning.

We as ordinary human beings must learn that we are all important in God's eyes and from the multifarious beauty of humanity we all matter. Our solvent tuning-fork with vibration should now culminate with our knowledge with a *Pianola and Piccolo* of reflection and vision as one. We must learn with our *psychological moment* consistently conveying our wisdom with knowledge and understanding. However, through mankind's existence upon this Planet of beauty we have still not understood truth.

We must now begin to understand the *whole picture* as an individual being of the *Universe* and the accumulation of knowledge and purpose with life. We must now begin to understand the beauty of our heavenly connection and absolve with life. We must now begin to understand the availability to all people who wish to enlighten their lives and *lighten* the load! Our *Psaltery of the medieval* will be psalmody of virtuous intent and *virtuoso* of melodious unification. In a nutshell, we will grow and blossom our truth into reality and reasoning. We will understand the complete workings of mind, body and spirit with life and our *instructions* from Heaven will bring us all celestial joy.

Yes, this book is to uplift our truth into the here and now of everyday living and to unite with realism and belief in the virtues of assimilations about fact or fantasy. Our hearts will rejoice with the learning and understanding of God, Angels, Masters, Mistresses and life. We can appease our downfalls with love and light bringing absolve to our fellowship, friends, family, loves and Earth.

From this our journey begins and only you as the individual will decide what is fact, truth and fantasy.

A NOTE FROM THE AUTHOR

....

Elizabeth Jane Parker 2012

....

The transcript of this work is not of the norm with spiritual assignation. The works contained are not about me as an individual. These writings are divination through astrophysics coalescing through *phenomenal conception* and spiritual alliance. All elements of biology and metaphysical transition have brought reality and reason from another dimension.

Of course there are many practitioners and theories surrounding spirituality. However, this work is not about fortune telling or systems of career making profit. This work is a *primeval agenda* with metaphysical absorption. Through seeing and understanding our Earth through bio diversity and teleology voices from another dimension I have been able to connect. *In a nutshell*, it is a votary of communication from divine persons who have lived and died through understanding scholastics within *Divine Discernment* and perspicuous philosophies about love, honour and truth.

For me personally, as Elizabeth, it has been both exciting and sometimes confusing to understand what is happening. As an *amanuensis for spiritual people* I have somehow emerged as intelligent student and studiously found an understanding with *God and his Holy Angels*. From this proselyte conversion my belief in God and the wonderful aspect of life's teachings has been elevated into one of realism. I now believe and understand my lessons as an individual. However, to explain to others what has happened is one of nascence and fervour about the reality of God.

The natural world is now a focus for us all with the realities and sustainability for the preservation of all life and wonder. Humanity is becoming more materialistic and with this comes loss of resources and loss of habitat. Great concern for our future is now in the balance. We as humanity have forsaken many things along the road of material growth and from this eventually we may lose the essence of sustainability and life forever. At present our limitations seem unreal and expansion with economy and growth brings great cost to our environment. Our unrealistic expectations within a world of limitation seem endless. So metaphorically speaking we need *"an audit for our calculus with evolution."* We all need to take responsibility both for ourselves and our Earth.

This book will speak to you as the individual who reads it. Many people from another dimension have given a voice for us in life. And from this you will find a pathway with a different perspective. I hope you enjoy and learn from the great *Masters and Angels* in Heaven who have taught me about the wonder and learning of life itself.

The Holy Trinity is Love, Honour and Truth...

Our pathways are a directive with wisdom when we truly believe in the realism of God our Father and Earth our Mother of life. The functioning with virtue is recognition of Holy Trinity and the realism of life and journey without delusion, dishonour and malcontent. Realism is our lives with virtuous intent. Reality is cognitive understanding of our truth. Heaven will come to Earth once we find our salvation with the Seven Sacraments of Virtue, Strength, courage, wisdom, compassion, love, honour and truth.

The Holy Bible is a great asset for our learning and projection with life and reasoning. From the pages of history we can appreciate the wonderful messages of the Holy Word. We all consign to the teachings of God with Virtue once we learn to understand the messages contained within the Holy Sacraments.

Elizabeth Jane Parker 2012.

Acknowledgement and Thanks

This book is dedicated to Michael, my husband and best friend with deep affection and love. Also, we would like to mention the dedication and hard work of the modern day "Freemasons." We would like to be "upstanding" and celebrate their own dedication to our God and Creator and the attributes of charity and generosity for many people who are in need of assistance and financial aid. Through our modernistic era we can commend them for their loyalty, love and kindness. Through the channels of virtue and affirmation to our God we can honour them all.

SPIRITUAL DYNAMICS

....

Elizabeth Jane Parker 2011

....

We *as humanity are in truth Cosmic Entrancement and Learned Philanthropic beings as biology and confinement within time and space. Our union with Heaven and Earth is a miracle within the spectrum of Universal Transition and life. How do we believe this through life, reason and intelligence? How do we unite and prosper as one and understand our diacritical eventuality through biological containment as a mortal being of the Universe? Simply and basically how and why can we metaphorically portray our Messianic belief and that of all other fellowship and responsibility upon this wondrous planet? How as humanity do we live with honour, humility, love, truth and compassion?*

The ethnological reasoning and aspect of astrophysics is a simple characteristic of philanthropy finding a passage through the Labyrinth of Elemental Reasoning and Life. The propulsion of aerodynamics is one of simple understanding and humility. Humility is another lesson for spiritual unification and learning spheres with time and space uniting with our truth. Our truth with life and Earth is to seek and discover positivism as a biological being. The format of life is cherishing our challenges as one with time and reality. Thus, to seek and find the treasures of Heaven, we all need to learn and maintain our natural law of spiritual essence within the confines of biological transition. *Through maintenance and virtue our navigation with achromatic transference is recognised through opalescent opportunity and preternatural with past primeval existence. Our origins within the Universe are unilaterally connected as an intelligent species within our World, Earth. How do we find reality and belief in our one God with respect and existence? In truth we as humanity have yet to believe in the human race as a divine and understanding phenomenon.*

Through each and every person discovering self-belief with virtue, honour and humility our journey with time can evolve into a spiritual reality. The Universal conception with the Spiritual Evolution Event can bring us all who love and cherish our world and philanthropy into a mega spectrum of macroscopic magnetisms' with Angels and truth. Through the concept of time and space procreating each and every molecule of humanity and life we live, learn and understand with virtuous reasoning and energy. Through the elemental changes of our planetary connection and the Universe within our observations towards planetarium space and time, we begin to understand our spiritual astrophysics with matter. Thus, we bring many voices into the arena of learning, listening and observation.

Through understanding our truth and virtue we can formulate our lives with all positive energies. The strength of positive mind-set with virtue brings our individual purpose into alignment with earth and her in the moment sphere. Through the velocity and universal unification with all learning spheres throughout the world and connection, we journey with the placement of reality and heavenly construction teaching us all to wonder and attenuate our current world of dilemma. The question is, does this formulate an interest to all of mankind for a better future?

The consequence of eternal change is progression with containment being at one with the Universe. Our Universe is unimaginable power. This power belongs to us all with learning and knowledge understanding love, light, honour, truth and beauty. We, as fellowship must disallow our darkness to dictate our passage with life. Through understanding the unnatural power of darkness we can evolve with reasoning evolution, recognising and dispersing negative forum with love but moving our journey forward with honour. This is the test of our journey to recognise and understand our weaknesses with forgiveness and absolve. Thus, our soul will lighten each and every step we take on Earth.

The Earth knows her history. She is a permanent truth. Her changes have brought destruction and cataclysmic events. However, her beauty and life force are eternal. We as human beings must understand her heartbeat with time and change and that of our own. This heartbeat is the journey, transition and connection with ancient memory. This memory is divine progression by mathematical and geology with change. Time allows change. This is a simple explanation for a complicated and mystical journey around the sun. The emphasis upon us all is to listen, learn and procreate our virtues with our planet.

Thus, our journey begins with truth.

OWNERSHIP WITH AUGMENTATION & CREDENCE

....

Part One

....

THE EVENING HAS COME

....

Elizabeth Jane Parker

....

Time has set and the evening has come
The story of one day is now undone
What was the answer upon our quest?
Did we seek our life's request?
From early dawn, the space in-between
Our journey today has now been

Did we value the day of gift
Did we see our life uplift?
The plans and purpose of each moment timed
Has our journey completely assigned?
Will our memory treasure the day?
From spiritual experience no time to delay
The gift of life to live and learn
From dawn to dusk we do return
Our intelligence provides,
Unconscious retained
Our wisdom aspires to be contained
Into our dreams our life unfolds
Refreshing our memory for stories untold

The beautiful evening brings birds in song
They tell the night there is no wrong
Their eco story has given them this time
Under the stars and moon will shine
The peaceful essence for us to absorb
The message of spiritual essence explored

Birds foraging for food in the garden today
They bring entertainment and a free display
Of the natural world in our garden to be
Beneficially abundant for all to see
To appreciate our life with the wonder around
The Earth and life giving us sound
Flying creatures and birds upon the wing
With eloquent beauty they will sing
Ecology merging within the spectrum
Motivation and survival, diverse collection
Observing the smallest miracle about
Their sustenance maintained essentially devout

The Feathers of an Angel, a message obtained
The knowledge of God to be maintained
The Angels abide into the night
The upturns and absorption, they will unite
All around us they permeate our lives
Despite unseeing with our own eyes
They exist for us all upon Earth's sphere
Gaining from love, eternally here

We all know God within our hearts
The reality of living ends and restarts

Each morning we awaken
Refreshed and to know
That we all belong to God and go
About our lives with a strong belief
That downturn and upsides can bring relief
That we are a miracle derived from a light
The eternal giving of God's might

Symbolic meaning from the Sun descends
The Evangelical picture recommends
With realism and Holy Scripture allowing a gift
From the ascension of knowledge to uplift
Our soaring spirit along the way
Gaining momentum with spirit today
Go into dreams of what can and will evolve
Our life's journey with God revolves
Love is the answer always with truth
Believing and knowing without reproof
We live and learn each precious inception
With God's grace and living conception
Our journey with time to relate
We give prayers to update
Our love
Our Honour
Our truth

For Ever Amen

CHAPTER ONE

WHAT IS INTELLIGENCE?

....

"The reasoning of our lives is to follow our virtue without false pride and revelation about God and truth. Through learning and understanding knowledge of the Heavens we all find the reality of life. Through our determination to follow a path of light with education brings us all to know the meaning of reality and reason through life and journey."

Elizabeth Jane Parker

....

The *upside of life is indeed a journey with wisdom.* This alone is not the diversity of being but the many other aspects of spiritual and biological assignment with life. For as a being, the challenges we face is with valour and virtue as our guide. What is virtue, we may ask? Virtue is the treasure we are all born with. Virtue is the way we follow with strong foundations. To learn and understand these foundations is the truth with virtuous intent and motivation. Is this easy in a modern world of darkness versus light? Do we understand dark energies and the positive and negative balance of spiritual reasoning? The roots of Heaven will grow for us all when we simply see and live with honest vision and reality. We simply focus upon the realities of life but understand that our journey is about challenge and virtue combining our source with wisdom.

How exactly are we inspired by life? We all have different perspectives and reasoning without families, work, play and gift. We all have different interests and diverse aspirations. We all need different things from life. Our mind, body and spirit rely upon sustainability with *bio diversity and bio chemistry* with superstructure and availability.

Our mind, body and spirit are in truth a miracle of creation through Cosmological Principle and compounds with light and dark energies theatrically and mathematically gravitational with cosmic expansion. So, to explain about life and journey: our unique position with *the Universe* is about divine science and belief with sight, sound, vibration, knowledge, aspirations, chemistry and truth. We are but small beings of intelligence. From time and motion we learn and grow through bio diversity and bio chemistry, the geographic spaces within our planet Earth. Our body and soul is but a small part of chemical engineering with imperceptible changes and evolution through space and time with the realities of life. From this as a species of marvel we ask about the realities of Angels and God.

However, from this our explanation with intelligence again is an eternal mystery to us all. Intelligence is unseen by matter so how in *realism do we explain the reality of an unseen Universe beyond biological comprehension and believability?*

Our biological functioning and brain formation is based upon modern-day philosophy and the schooling we have through curriculum. The diversity of teaching methods and availability to learn often digresses through individuality and opinion. As yet, communication with parallel Universes is a theory and not as yet understood or believed by influential *Scientists and Sceptics* and from this the believable requires proof. However, intelligence is the unseen phenomena they use as a tool with aspiration and research for their scientific reasoning. The question here is where does intelligence form? What exactly is our imagination? How do we as a human species learn from biology and diversity?

Belief for many in God is a belief in a simple fact, that is about the *light of good*. However, from this we bring to bear the message of dark energies. How indeed do we learn from them? If there was only light within our *Universe* we would in truth not exist. From the darkness we can eventually see light with reasoning and wisdom and thus we all can find strength from determination and virtue balancing our monochromatic energies with life. For *out of darkness comes light*. Our focus and wisdom become the adventure with life when we simply learn to believe in the wonder of life itself despite the ups and downs we experience. From simply learning to see with our virtue is the test of our journey with God and reasoning. Intelligence is the greatest gift of all life with our great *Mother Earth*. From this the bio diversity and chemistry we all live with teaches us about *"the eye of learning."* Through unseen atoms and chemistry together with the truth of wisdom is to know the symbolic meaning of *greater knowledge* for us all that has grown from the seed of life.

Our lives bring many lessons with our virtue and wisdom together. Thus is the beauty of biological reasoning and the reasoning of spiritual essence, we bring our journey to understand our own truth but we cannot live our lives for another's truth. *We shine our light with reality and reasoning upon the earth to bring comfort but align our spirituality and biology with compassion and love. The teachings of The Way involve us all.*

....

Anabolism with genetics is just the beginning with our journey with time. Through the growth of our learning and lessons with life, the pragmatic astrophysics with life accumulates with our virtuous intentions superseding each challenge and beset us all upon our passage with time. Understanding is just the beginning each and every day of our life with mortality and light together. The challenges that beset us all are about seeking, understanding and absolving all misfortune and disrespect along the road of enlightenment. Thus, finding forgiveness and love brings our spiritual assignation into alignment with all things of virtue and love.

Elizabeth Jane Parker 2010.

Psalm 92

It is a good thing to give thanks unto the Lord,
And to sing to thy name, o most high:
To show forth thy loving kindness in the morning,
And thy faithfulness every night,
Upon an instrument of ten strings, and upon thy psaltery,
Upon the harp of a solemn sound
For thou, lord has made me glad through thy work.

CHAPTER TWO

THE GYROSCOPE OF LIFE AND METAPHYSICAL CHANGE

....

"The simplicity of truth is our ligature when we refuse to use the boundaries set by virtue. Understanding divine discernment is about our truth and absolve. Thus, we give our love to all fellowship through understanding with compassion all dishonour by moving forward without looking back. This is the deep test of our soul and virtue."

Elizabeth Jane Parker

....

The *obbligato of our lives with fellowship* is to learn and formulate our understanding with truth. Through the metaphysics and transition of everyday living, we bring our truth to integrate with all other energies of life. Through our life we will often question the motives and communicative procedures of others and their thoughts and opinions. Through our wisdom with reaction our blessings with life are taught to understand that we are *all different* in life, but united as one within Heaven. Thus, through our passage with life we find many differences of thought and belief. Through this concept we use our wisdom to *listen* with compassion but to acknowledge our status quo and move on with our life.

Our federal teachings with life are to understand our sentinels within Heaven will arbitrate our truth through a

25

system of *self-analysis*, when our conscience becomes *clear* through honour and not dishonour. Our conscience is very much assimilated with our metaphysical transition. The wheel of time is ever spinning with our truth, However, when our vibrations weaken with dishonour, we lose momentum through time and space with reality and reasoning. This lesson brings us *in the moment* acceptance to collide with our telegraphy with truth and honour being at one.

As spiritual beings we can all learn and grow. However, life brings the challenges to our metaphysics with emotion and reaction. Emotion and reaction as we have explained is very powerful. Through the concept of life and reasoning we can become embroiled with the powers of dark emotive stance and lose our status quo with reasoning and wisdom. This is the strong test of our journey with time. How do we contravene the negative pull of emotion and life? Our body of light is greatly tested and our virtues with conscience and consciousness become one with negative lure. Our natural vibrations bring our bearing once more to understand that our passage with life is the challenge to our virtue. Thus, our adrenalin with learning and downfall brings our status into more energy and light through the electrodynamics of change. To remain within the confines of disappointment will bring fatigue. Fatigue can be dispelled with our positive mind-set asserting control with love and truth. Thus, our truth is the metaphysical spin of our life with grounding energies reaching up to our higher learning within heavenly spheres. Through our belief in God and his virtues we can find our passage once more with the natural spin of time and our Earth. How do we learn and alleviate our misgivings with time?

Love and honour are brought with our truth and transition upon the wheel of life, thus, understanding the dilemmas of many we bring our compassion and wisdom to bear downfall with love. We learn to override negativity with devotion to our passage. We learn that our way is ordained from *The Heavens*. We learn to move our wheel into momentum with forgiveness and love. *Thus, our Angelic protection will assimilate with our truth and we learn to love our life with vitality, reasoning and virtue.*

Our soul is deeply connected to the eternal vibrations of God, many people may find this impalpable to modern-day thinking and realism. The availability of proof is necessary for belief. The idea of Seraph Angels and hierarchal dominions is but a fantasy to modern-day Scientists. So – how do we prove the wonders of healing, knowledge and unseen phenomena with truth? In this we are not theoretical as species. We are not fantasy. We have all grown through Earth and her journey around the Sun. We are real and from this we can find our deep understanding with life and reasoning with truth, belief and wonder of our very existence within the spectrum of life.

Angels' Decree

Respect all Virtue of metaphysical finesse
Thus, our masters of destiny bless
Spiritual containment with bodily glow
Understanding our Heavens and Earth to know
That deep in our hearts the wonder of time
To karmic truth we seek to define

The smell of the ocean heightens our senses
Continued love always commences
The whispers of the wind
Touches our hair
Knowing our purpose is always to care
That Earth is so precious for all to enjoy
Our love for her treasures
Will always bring joy

Our journey with love we see with our eyes
The beauty of life is always the prize
Thoughts and messages
For Heaven and Earth
Our moments of time will bring us rebirth
To arise from the night
And bring a new day
God and his angels show us the way
Blessings of love
Our kindred of all
Angelic Renaissance can ne'er be small
Collectively choosing to live with a dream
Today and forever we seek to redeem
Our love of God and Goddess as one
Loving each moment that has begun

Forever with love
Forever with God

CHAPTER THREE

THE HYPERTEXT OF KARMIC WEAVE

....

"Our lives will grow into graceful acceptance when we all begin to take responsibility for our own actions and speech. Thus, understanding our transition with Angels and God brings us all to love and honour each other and our earthly vibrations with life."

Elizabeth Jane Parker 2010.

....

Our *symbiosis with life* is the confusing mechanism and complication we all experience with wisdom. The teaching of our journey and passage often brings us to formulate opinions which are not actually teaching us about life and her treasures. We as *human beings* have through centuries of learning not absolved the turmoil or evil that we have created. Thus, the enormity of this aspect seems unrealistic to many modern-day thinkers. The thoughts and reality of many people is not to believe and to remain unenlightened with life. Through the concept of holding on to emotive stance and yesterday's downfall they fail to move in unison with all of life and our Earth. Thus, this is the reality and reasoning of our modern day world and the mistakes of the past.

Felicitous thoughts and positive actions bring our being to a higher place when we feel peaceful and tranquil. How do we go about this? Our spiritual one seeks to bring our Earth into a higher vibration for all. This may seem impossible to many disbelievers, however, to believe in God and the wonder of life is simply about virtue. Understanding our mathematical convergence with life assimilates our *Angelic Geometry, and the time aspect of our life through our Chakra System* and integral calculus. This we discussed in *"Voices from Heaven."* Our learning with heaven is the objective of our life to understand our passage and downturns and to bring about a higher promotion with astrophysics with confirmation of our belief with virtue, love and honour.

There are many people who dishonour us, however, their passage through life is about learning too. Through their learning they will bring negative charms to our *doorstep.* How do we dispense our own and listen to theirs? Our honour to our brethren is the key to finding our own truth and virtue. These keys open many doors with the strength, compassion, wisdom and courage of the enlightenment process. *The quadrilateral assimilation with Angelic divining is the practice and understands these virtues.* They abide for us all to acknowledge, accept and allow their intervention with prayer, affirmation and request.

Of course, we may meditate to bring peace, however, the solvency of our future as one is to seek the treasures of spiritual life through our belief, honour, truth and love of all things. This is our life. This is our way. To find the wonder of life and belief will be taught to us all through our karmic weave and transition.

CHAPTER FOUR

EXPUNGING AND EXTRICATION OF MISUNDERSTANDINGS

....

"And I set my face unto the Lord God, to seek prayer and supplications, with fasting and sackcloth, and ashes: and I prayed unto the LORD my God, and made my confession." - Daniel 9

....

Our *creative aspirations for daily prayer and life are a gift to us all.* Our realisations of our experiences everyday bring to our fellowship and conformity the aspirations for tomorrow.

We are all on a mission with *God our Father in Heaven and our Mother Earth.*   Each and every pattern of our karmic weave is brought through our spiritual migration through life. For our status quo and transitional footsteps through the maze allows us all to reason and understand the mistakes of yesterday bring us a truth for tomorrow. We all belong to reality and reasoning our virtues, downfalls and darkness. For man and woman have a biological commitment with truth. This truth is to allow our passage and faith with reasoning to follow our natural intuition and perspective with choice, wisdom and love for our heavenly mother and father with life. Our footsteps follow a passage with understanding that we are the *children of Heaven and Earth* with life.

31

Through our labyrinth with kinematics our healthy mind-set will transform and grow with our intelligence understanding our connection with each other and all of life with the beauty of virtuous reasoning. Our beauty in life is to believe that we are all *in this together* and through *thick and thin* we utilize our monochromatic energies to balance our reasoning with life. We all have choice within our *free world* and despite Governments misleading us with untruths, we perform our incarnation with the knowledge that universally we are all brothers and sisters sharing our Planet with a hope. This hope is to transform our depleting world with *Spirit and Biology* as twins with a journey. Through this journey our connection with life reconnects our spirit and soul as a breathtaking experience with light and matter together.

Our biological blessings of the material dimension are extended through our journey into heavenly realms with our truth. Through every avenue we are blessed to believe that our journey will transform our misunderstandings into one of supernatural absolve and reasoning through the magic of forgiveness and translation. Deep within us all we know this but somehow through each and every generation our road has not brought us all to understand the spiritual message of our soul and that is to love and respect. *Thus, we must all bring our fellowship into the light with our metaphysics through each and every bend of life to stand our ground and understand the power of self-belief and contentment.*

Angels of God and light are everywhere. They abide for us to learn and understand our purpose with life and reason. The eternal knowledge is known to us all eventually, both from our *Heavens and Earth* as one. Thus, the treasures of life await us through our spiritual assignation with time and space. Our journey will once more perceive the essence and biological transformations of life as an adventure and beautiful story with history. However, we all need to respect honour and love our brethren and sisters with eternal knowledge and love.

Humility with Honour

The truth of light will not redeem reckless ignorance and denial of weakness. All seekers of truth and enlightenment must recognize the virtue and humility of forgiveness and apology. The love of Christ brings this message to all who seek the treasures of divine understanding. Our virtues with God embellish our beauty and light with the humility of learning. Humility and love bring our being into a better place when we recognise and realise our misunderstandings. Our misunderstandings will transcend into love with forgiveness and honour when we speak and become our truth.

Elizabeth Jane Parker
2010

CHAPTER FIVE

PRIDE OR PREJUDICE

....

Repent thee, for the kingdom of heaven is at hand."

St. Matthew 3

....

Weaving *our way through the avenues of time and space* brings us many *crosses to bear* with dishonour and untruth. The question is how do we overcome this? Many people have problems with thoughts and metaphysics weaving *negative charm* into the reality of everyday life. How does the power of light overcome the dishonour? We are all impermanent and we all have our grounding weaknesses with virtue. The question through our journey with life is how to extricate and explain our own truth with reasoning.

Dishonour and untruth is a message from ownership to *release* the energies following our path. Our thought processes are indeed part of our individuality and virtue. Consequently, through the avenues of purpose our truth must alleviate and dissipate the *annoyance* we are all apt to feel. The lesson of pride is to *listen* to our intuition and feel the vibration of truth. The vibration of truth is to set free our mind-set with *love*. Yes, another lesson with compassion *is* love.

Compassion and false pride often confuse our status quo. Through compassion and pride working as one we find that our alignment with truth can deny our existence with monochromatic energies curtailing our nascent progress with light. *False pride* has many downturns with spiritual enlightenment processes. Through denial and untruth the ownership of an individual will not be able to seek and find their source. This sadness is the lure of ego and false pride. To understand our journey we must all recognize our weaknesses with pride and compassion as one. The journey with love is one of knowledge, affinity and truth accumulating through our connection with God. However, denial and weakness are the arbitrators of false pride and blindness to virtue through misconception and dishonour. To understand truth, our weakness can only be absolved with congruence, virtue and reasoning formulating and processing our metaphysics with forfeiting our pride and ego with *apology* and honour with graciousness and serenity.

Through the history of mankind, these lessons have been sadly overlooked. The wonder of life and reasoning is the journey we all undertake. To speak with honour and courtesy is the diplomatic reasoning with Angels and God. Through the works and knowledge of our source we can all find the beauty of reasoning our weakness and overcoming our false pride with virtue. Prejudicial untruths become one of dishonour to our bearing and to all others through the *Divine Purpose* of our lives and understanding with God. Through God's word and that of our individual status quo upon the *Earth* and spherical learning we can all find peace, tranquillity and purpose with our journey with understanding our God and his Angels.

Understanding is the requisition of our bearing with life when we all overcome our blindness and false pride. False pride is a difficult lesson for us all. Thus, through dissipation and love to our Earth and her treasures we can all find our purpose and transition with eternal forgiveness.

Elizabeth Jane Parker 2012.

Divine Reasoning

Elizabeth Jane Parker 2012.

The trust of the Universe must be perceived, acknowledged and earned through "Divine Reasoning." Yes, we can all connect at periods of our life with Angelic assistance, however, to learn from Angelic Realms and to dissipate small energies we all need to acknowledge "The Congregation" of virtue and humility as one. The fragmentation through life is to feel with reaction and thus sometimes act without wisdom. Thus, without wisdom we cannot see the beauty of life. Our blindness causes loss of momentum and we feel dissatisfied and disappointed. Through our disappointment and downfall the progression of growth will stagnate until we reason our ill-will with foundation and our Mother Earth.

Spiritual Essence will merge with others who also seek to "hold on" to their delusion and thus the messages of negative charm remain with vengeance. Vengeance is a weak energy surrounded by darkness. This is the sadness of Earth and Nirvana and the energies of life. We simply misunderstand our journey. To release our spiritual darkness is to forgive and to move on with love. Again, our lesson with love is humility, absolve and compassion. Our lessons with virtue will bring our understanding into a better place through metaphysical transience with downfall. Through the combination of apology, forgiveness and humility, we become one with our brethren and sisters of life.

CHAPTER SIX

THE CONGREGATION OF REALITY AND "THE SEE"

SPIRITUAL EVOLUTION EVENT

....

"The See of life is about realism and belief transforming our metaphysics with virtue and love. The See of life is about rectification and virtue. The See of life is about humanity and love combining intelligences with respect. The See of life is about God, Earth and transition."

Elizabeth Jane Parker2010

....

As *a spiritual essence of modernistic transitions* our abilities to see through the judgemental opinions and often endogenous difficulties of reasoning, brought to us all through our media, education systems, propaganda and all powerful tools of communication, as a spiritual essence of ancient prophesies and transitions, how can we all realistically move into another dimension where peace and tranquillity absolve our downturns with reality and reasoning?

We are aware of the *"doom and gloom"* predominating our global transitions into the light. We are aware that many people disagree. We are aware of dogmatic opinion and fundamentalism. However, how can we as spiritual essence return to our origins with virtue and divinity? How do we learn through the *minefield* of dilemmas and life?

The message of *freedom and light* is to look with ownership and clarification that *all will be well* with the aspect of hope, transition and unification with people who wish to truly associate and learn to grow with the word of God. God speaks to us all through our journey with life when we *observe, listen and reform* our religions and creeds into universal respect for each other. As human beings we all need to honour all others who diversify their belief. Thus, through our forbearance and way with the light of reasoning we all become *way showers* with time and space with reality.

The 'SEE' of life is forbearance with virtue and to understand that we are all gifted from God. We are all upon a journey of learning. This learning is to look, listen and feel our vibration with Heaven, but to walk the path of life with joy, knowledge, humility and love. Our journey is to seek and acknowledge that we all belong to God. Yes, he is personal. He teaches us all through life and reasoning. Pre-Christian values were through another dimension of learning. This learning was as sacred as we are today. Our judgement and values have gradually been dispersed and thus the saying *"united we stand and divided we fall."*

Mankind has the beauty of diversity and knowledge with wisdom if he so chooses. Mankind has the breath and beauty of biology. Mankind has the grace and beauty to transform his *ill-gotten* passage with a damaged planet of magnificent beauty. Mankind has the ability to see and learn about our spiritual passage with humility, virtue and honour. Together with love we can all 'SEE' our World in all of her splendour. We can all feel her vibration with that of our own. We can all honour and obey the laws of nature, sustenance, comfort and love. *We can all learn.*

CHAPTER SEVEN

THE REALITY OF CHANGE
AND IMAGINATION

....

*"The eyes of the LORD preserve knowledge, and he overthrows
the words of the transgressor."*

Prov. 23

....

The *fundamentalism* of change is simply to find our belief with
God and his Holy Angels. To actually bring about changes and
reasoning of our lives is to understand the Universe and the
reasoning of God. Through God we can all find our truth with
life and bring our being to a higher vibration with trust. Trust of
the universe is to seek with forbearance and love, the attributes
of our sometimes severe choices and downfalls with life.
Through each and every downturn, we encumber our lives if we
disbelieve in the attributes of divinity. The treasures and reality
with God teach us all to align our truth with our Planet and her
life force.

Imagination is a tool which aligns with our consciousnesses,
and with all aspects of our everyday thoughts and sight with life.
To understand our imagination is one of learning and transition.
Through life there are many who misunderstand spirituality and
truth. They seek all avenues to find the treasures of *Divine
Understanding* but fail to understand God's reasoning with virtue,

love and trust. Through these simple words we can find a solution to our disbelief and anxiety with confused messages and teachings. God and truth is about the Holy Angels dissipating and sending negative energies back to the Universe with True Love and virtue. However, each and every person upon our Planet must learn to absolve their reasoning.

Our light is the fundamental passage with virtue and change once we all understand our mortality and the immortality of our soul incarnate. Through bringing our incarnation and spiritual essence into our soul we allow the beauty and wonder of universal transition and glory of our Angels into the highest realm and vibration. As we have discussed previously, *Arch Angels* are the sentinels of virtue and vibration with intelligence and learning. Through their channel only, can all be allowed to enter the realms of Angelic Healing and understanding with God?

We must all learn and understand our transitions. These are the attributes of seeking, finding and maintaining our status quo with Angelic Realms. Through spirituality and God we can all find our treasures and the gold of Divine Understanding. However, our lessons and choices with virtuous intention often bring people to disregard and disbelieve divine message. Often denial and retribution disallow their growth with the elements of emotion and downfall. Anger, bitterness and fear often bring people to mistrust virtue. They seek but cannot find the love and blessings of their journey. Thus, attempting to discharge deep feelings of distress and fear bring them into a dark place whereby they blame God and his virtues. This disrespect is through mind-set undergoing imaginative delusions about truth. The message of reality and reasoning is to understand God and his Angels. This understanding is about clearance of karma with bringing our virtues and truth into alignment with forgiveness and belief. This belief allows our transition to alleviate the grief, darkness and negative charms of downfall.

People often misunderstand that the third eye and the "*The Eye of Learning.*" The Eye of Learning is Nirvana and the Angelic forces awaiting transition through the avenues and journey with life and reasoning. The wisdom of truth and love are the attributes this eye sees. Nature and formation are us all. To disassociate our reasoning and individual karma with misunderstanding will bring our being and life away from the "*sight*" of Divinity and Holy Angels. They await us all finding our passage with truth and their intervention with reality and reasoning, and the Earth and her movements around the Sun. The power and geometrics of love and light can only be found through this eye. All of nature and life forces with Divinity have understood this eye. Thus, we must all now begin to understand that our changes are constantly seeking Angelic assistance with our divine purpose with life.

Ownership, Nirvana and Earth are the attributes of our individual formation and blessings with God. Thus, our journey is ordained with each other and life. Through progressive teachings from Heaven we will all eventually find our treasures and the "*gold*" of understanding with Angels and God.

CHAPTER EIGHT

THE EXCURSION WITH TIME
VICTIM OF CIRCUMSTANCE
OR CHOICE

....

"Speak not in the ears of a fool: For he will despise the wisdom of thy words. Remove not from the old landmark, and enter not into the land of the fatherless."

Prov. 23

....

Our *mind-set promotion* is one of self-awareness and consciousnesses emerging through time and space. Understanding the geographies and movement with reality our inbuilt charisma brings us a choice of reasoning. One of the lessons through our life is to assimilate our thoughts and actions with biology and time. The consequence of this takes us on a journey with experience. Through our experience we can all observe and rectify our imbalances with darkness. Darkness is our continual test with life and reasoning. Darkness can teach us lessons but to disperse the consequences we all need to acknowledge our weaknesses with time and space. This brings ego into the arena of life. Thus, despite our goodness and prosperity with time many people deny their "*shadow*" aspect of learning. Through our shadow self we can dissemble all of our wonderful experiences with doubt and denial. Thus, scepticism creeps into our soul incarnate and the *"light"* of reasoning can elude us.

Many people deny the beauty and wonder of fellowship. The questions of mortality bring many painful aspects of our journey with beauty and light. Thus, through our lessons with downfall, many people cannot find their strength and courage to grow again. The ups and downs bring confusion to their light. Thus, the reasons for humanity and eternal spirit are lost within the confines of their mortal being and the treasures they seek remain *lost*. We can all choose to be victims with life. Thus, through our journey we fail to see and know the beauty of God and his Angels. We fail to believe that good is better than bad. We fail to understand the clarity of virtuous intent.

Each day of our lives are the blessings and magic of the heavens, but through delusional imagination many people live each day with doubt, denial and sometimes shame of the inability to see, learn and know about cosmic transference and the reality of time accumulation with learning and knowledge. They fail to see the learning aspects of their spirit life upon our *Divine Mother* and her natural nurture with change and absolve. God speaks to us all through the channels of humility, love, trust, truth and gift. Yes, we all have gift and the learning aspect of time within the beautiful sphere of Earth and her own journey around the Sun. The geography of evolution is ever changing and so must we. We fail as a human species to realise our connection with through the Earth and her magnitude and beauty. Despite her limitations through the vast areas of space she gives us all life.

Life is the learning curve of reality and reasoning. From birth to demise we fill the time and space allotted to us all. We all know this but still across the sphere of Earth we all fail to understand our *Heaven and Earth* connection. We fail to see the beauty of our incarnation and healing aspect of learning and absolve. We fail to transcend the virtues and beauty of life and spiritual assignation with time and space. Thus, until we all fully appreciate the *Divine Message* of life we will not fulfil our destiny. Through all divine messages we can learn and grow with our God and Holy Angels. We all have a choice and determination hidden within our soul. Thus, to seek and find the treasures of life through sacred learning brings us back home. Home is where the heart is. Our heart seeks life only to experience all heavenly connection with God.

CHAPTER NINE

NAUTICAL NAZARENE AND QUINTESSENCE

....

"And right to them that find knowledge. Receive my instruction and not
silver, and knowledge rather than choice gold. For thy wisdom is better
than rubies, and all that is to be desired not to be compared with it."

Prov. 9

....

The *Christ Light of reasoning* is a reason. The reason of truth and
fellowship formulates our understanding with reality and God.
Through God and his essence with Mother Earth we all
experience life. The essence of change of virtue "allows" our
ship and vessel of life to negotiate *the high seas* with the inter-
planetary helmsmen and reasoning. Our ship upon the waters
of reality and reasoning understand the elements of change and
virtue. To live and learn with all aspects of diversion and
teachings, our eternal knowledge and growth aspire to our
belief and transition with God.

When we survive the *stormy seas* and ups and downs of life's
adventures, our understanding with self-belief brings our status
and bearing into *Angelic Realms* with virtue. Through
organising our thoughts and metaphysics with reality we can
all deny the reasoning of ego and delusionary imagination.
Jesus Christ brought to us all the learning of this. His
negotiations as *a Great Teacher* were simply through his belief in

virtue, love and truth. As a man of supernatural healing he brought the beauty and the wonder of *The Universe* into all people who understood his message. Of course, we all honour and obey our religious beliefs and to deny all others is the sin of dishonour and disrespect. The aspect of our learning is to acknowledge and accept that our individual aspirations will always differ with our brethren and fellowship with life. Self-belief and virtue belong to us all. Through the teachings of Christ we can all appreciate and love our brother and sisters despite our differences in belief. Thus is the lesson of humility and understanding the virtues of our passage with light!

The light of humanity is the beauty and blessings from God our father. He teaches us all eventually to seek light and redemption. Across the holy waters of time, shall we be ever loved through the written words of God our father in heaven? We rejoice in the sanctity of life and reasoning our virtues with the written word through ancient and modern messages. May we all be blessed through understanding and creating our virtues through to the next millennia!

And straightway he constrained his disciples to get into the ship, and to go to the other side unto "Bethsaida", while he sent away the people. And when he had sent them away, he departed into the mountain to pray. And when even was come, the ship was in mid sea, and he alone on the land. He saw them toiling and rowing, for the wind was contrary to them, and about the fourth watch of the night he cometh to them, walking upon the sea, and would have passed them. But they saw him walking upon the sea, they supposed it was spirit, and cried out for they all saw him, and were troubled. And immediately he talked with them and said, be of good cheer, it is I, be not afraid. And he went up to them into the ship, and the wind ceased, and they were sore amazed in themselves beyond measure and wondered.

Our ship upon the waters of time often leaves us with dilemma and thus the feet of our Lord came to us all when we were suffering and in need. His spiritual beauty and example gave us all reasoning with God and our Mother Earth. From symbolism and our Holy Bible we can understand the teachings of virtue and love.

Our journey with life often causes us to confuse our faith with desire. Desire often blinds our reality and imagination and the stormy seas of life bring us often into despair from our desires and wrongful imagination. Time and space are us all bringing our ship into harbour and understanding our faith and not desires with life. Our faith is the hardest lesson for us all to understand when our lives become a difficult encounter. Self-righteous overtures and judgemental opinions bring us to bear another cross with ill intent. Thus we again fail to see the beauty of God and our Mother of truth.

God is truthful but forgiving all downfalls with true love of all things. Thus, through enlightenment we can pass on our love and forgiveness for all. Blessings are our world of one and into the future we will embrace our truth and that of all others seeking divine love and light.

Life is...

The *Adventure, Wisdom is the journey, Love is the answer and truth is our path. Our journey with time is the aspiration of hope over adversity. Through the challenges of life we never look back. Always give blessings for downfalls but move on into life with courage. Truth of our foundations will bring us unto Heaven with the joy of learning overcoming distraction. We find our love and compassion absolving disappointments with focus and objectivity with life. Seeking our passage with time is the adventure of our Soul in Major. All components of strength, courage, wisdom, compassion, love, honour and truth become our salvation with learning. Our Mirror of Actuality is the way of God and truth understanding "Reality and Reasoning" with the SEE (spiritual evolution event) of time itself. We all have this if we find our foundations with virtue and Earth. Through this portal we truly find Heaven will unite with us all."*

Elizabeth Jane Parker 2012.

The Window of Time

Elizabeth Jane Parker

Sitting at the Window of Time
Watching the ocean so serene, so fine
The young gulls calling to Earth
The pale blue sky begins a new day
Begins rebirth,
Watching the clouds flowing through the sky,
A sky of mighty blessings, blessings so high,
The sea and land unite with peace
The gentle breeze
The gentle day
Awaiting for unfoldment
Awaiting for truth
Yesterday's journey begins with today

Karmic lessons and interplay
Peace and tranquillity alight on the waters of calm,
Blessings with quintessence and healing balm,
Awaiting the day
Awaiting for us
Pastel shades compose the palette
Colours define the horizon
Our eye paints the picture of hope
Without desire
Without greed
Without hate
For generations and Earth's condition
With beauty and light and definition
For the Earth and her riches
For Earth and her vibration
For Earth and her beauty
Lightens the day with clarification
Upon the tides of fate,
Scenes of florescence and orientation,
With silver rays across the sea
The wonder of evolution can be
With interest, love and reality
Our journey brings us to Burnham-on-Sea

A beautiful resort and spiritual entity
Seaside aspirations of holiday peace
Relaxing and friendly our stress to release
Like a bird in the sky,
Flying so high,
We enjoy the sun and gentle breeze
Walking graciously upon the Esplanade,

Chatting with companionship and serenade,
Of pleasure and living the joy that we seek
Our holiday of seeing throughout the week

A notice says upon the wall so pale,
Our **Lord Jesus of Israel**,
Placed his feet upon the sands of these shores
His spiritual journey as a boy,
With Joseph he came to this land,
His inspiration and thoughts are a mystery,
The light of Christ is one of history,
To know his presence is for all to share,
To know he came to give and care.
The Christ light of love, truth and honour to our One
Through his journey we feel uplifted,
He brought the message of all who are gifted
With belief and knowledge of truth and love,
To set our sins free
To believe in God
To believe in humanity
To believe in our future
The love of Christ was one of learning
Our truth
Our freedom
Our journey
Our hope

CHAPTER TEN

FOOTSTEPS THROUGH THE MAZE WITH REALITY WITH TIME

....

"I wisdom dwell with prudence and find out knowledge of witty inventions."

Prov. 9

....

The *maze of our lives*, through the concept of time and space, is simply one of learning, choice, freedom and love. Wisdom is to understand our humility and the knowledge we all seek through our individualism with reality and time.

Our perspective as an individual is one of learning, observing and believing in our ownership with truth. Truth is the treasure of life when we are permutated and accredit our path with self-awareness and evaluation with virtue. Our monochromatic energies and shadow aspect of learning is to bring our focus and clarification with life to understand, utilise *release* and forgive our fellowship. The opinions of many are the learning aspects and perspective of reasoning our truth and the motions of eternal movement with Earth and her spiritual essence with all things. Many people actually *fail* to understand that weakness can bring strength. Many people fail to recognize and explore their *shadow* aspect of learning with honouring truth with absolves.   Many people *choose* not to believe their ownership is connected with spirituality and the theism of science and reality as one. Thus, through controversial and differences, religions and God become one of *mismatch proportions*. Is this a truth during our modern age?

The transfiguration of the changes throughout our life is to seek and acknowledge, appreciate and choose our wisdom over the *shadow* side of our soul, and to simply understand the teaching process of darkness. The downside through misunderstanding darkness is that many people find their pride and belief in their individual journey as one of holier than thou, and fail to understand their journey with life as one of seeking the treasures of knowledge and wisdom and dispersing the malfunction of *shadow*.

The precipitous climb to reach higher awareness can be attained through understanding the simple attributes of respect and compassion. Through our lives we must recognize and realise our self-awareness as one of presentation, virtue and pro-action with truth. Our Earth moves systematically every day with her truth as a creator of opportunity for us all. Each and every person upon this planet has opportunity, choice and freedom of spirit when we understand our humility and tranquillity through spiritual assignation and knowledge.

Through the channels of sceptics and scientific reasoning, many people disbelieve the connection and attainment with higher knowledge. Thus, the self-belief and awareness aspect of their journey becomes one of *default* and without unison for the realities and truth of learning with *God and his Holy Angels*. Through the harrowing aspect of death, destruction and greed, their truth may follow the historic eventualities of *pride comes before a fall*. Thus is the structure of our modern world at present, the sharing and caring attribute of fellowship becomes one of sceptic credulous devotion to money and power. *The mountain of truth* becomes one of carrying excrescence to beauty and fails to climb within the Heavens of virtue, love and honour. Money and power take precedence over the love and honour to all brethren and sisters in need. Money and power become the delusion and irregularity with passage and truth.

Through grounding hydrostatics and quintessential journey with acknowledgement and pro-action with truth, the footsteps of humanity will lead us all to a higher vibration without greed, hate and dishonour. Through the elements of *pragmatic astrophysics* and time we can all find a beauty in life and feel without heart the sadness of our present-day existence but the hope and glory of change into virtuous reasoning with life and our future aspirations as spiritual and scientific revelation.

Be not thou envious against evil men,
Neither desire to be with them,
For their heart studies destruction,
And their lips talk of mischief.
Through wisdom is a house built,
And by understanding is it established,
And by knowledge chambers are filled
With all precious and pleasant riches
A wise man is strong,
Yea, a man of knowledge increases strength.

The Holy Bible

CHAPTER ELEVEN

NUMINOUS DEXTERITY

....

"A man shall be satisfied by the good by the fruit of his mouth."
Prov. 12

....

The *beauty of time and space* is augmented throughout our life by a simple acknowledgement. That acknowledgment is to believe in good. The good and bad of life are often dominated by *the bad* giving interest and domain over the fractious and disorientated aspects of our modern world. We of course understand the elements of darkness into light but darkness is not the answer to divination and truth, when we seek our treasures and loves of life.

To be, or not to be, constitutes the choices we have through physical and biological transience with life. Our little *acorn* grows with love, sustenance and care. Through living and experiencing the ups and downs with life's journey we indeed live to learn. This adage must be understood through the *New Age of Reasoning*. The sceptics of life perceive nature and reasoning as one of actuality and existence presenting *fact* over our unseen functioning with truth. However, the assignation with spiritual divination takes us all on our individual experiences with truth. Consequently, through our Earth and her journey within the Cosmos all of us are enabled to follow our star. That star is Earth, yes, simply and realistically we all live within her sphere and geometry, geography and graphics. Through assignation and learning with that of her journey we can all perceive and live our lives with knowledge. However, through the passing of time and the journey with life mankind has forgotten to see and understand through listening, observing and respect of our individualism and unification as one. So, many lessons to be learnt and understood bring our vibration to the highest level when we realise that our humility and wisdom are the attributes of divinity.

Many people fail to see, listen and know that through these avenues with truth, we all connect and reconnect our vibration with *The Masters of the Universe*. Their voices have brought our humanity from primitive to productive essences with life, but to respect and honour our humble foundations with higher knowledge, continuously updating and correcting our journey with time. We are all blessed with life through spiritual and biological existence. The miracles and wonder of life are apparent to us all through the power and belief of the Heavens when we all work with God and his followers, Angels and teachers.

The true power allocated to biology is one of a journey with continual learning. This learning is about the truth and beauty of our inner sanctum connecting with the outer realities of life. However, many people simply choose influence from others and fail to recognize and realise that we all learn from each other and our weakness, strengths and blessings with virtue. We all learn to attain greater knowledge through our inspiration from the heavenly source, when we truly believe and understand the virtue, love and honour of our lessons.

This is where love truly reigns. Admiration and respect bring us all to recognize that we are related in Heaven. For within

Heaven there is no desire or greed. In Heaven we all honour, respect and obey our God and the knowledge that has accumulated through Earth and her journey with life and spiritual essence. Power comes from the love within us all. Once we all understand the seven sacraments of virtue our heavenly vibration can come to us all. For Heaven and Earth unite through the breath and beauty of eternal knowledge and love.

We are bound to thank God always for you,
Brethren and Sisters, as is meet,
Because your faith grows exceedingly,
And the charity of every one of you all,
Abounds, so we can glory in you the churches
Of God for your patience faith in all of
Your persecutions and tribulations that
You endure: which is a manifest token of the
Righteous judgement of God, that you may
Be worthy of the Kingdom of God.

The Holy Bible

Prayer

Elizabeth Jane Parker 2012

Through our eternal Father and Mother of life
May we proceed with illustrious love and virtue?
Through all eternal knowledge may we abide?
By the Covenants of Heavenly realms
Bring forth the love and integrity of wisdom,
Bring forth the idealism of blessings and life,
As one understanding with God
Through avenues of fellowship and reasoning
Bring forth the knowledge of respect
Bring forth the beauty of courage
Bring forth the learning of strength
Bring forth the wonder of compassion.
The pyramidal aspect of the seven sacraments
With the Divine Three
Love, honour and truth
Bring forth the stairway unto Heaven
Into the realms of understanding our light
For we are truly blessed with truth and love
Through the virtues and honour of the
Holy Covenants

Amen

CHAPTER TWELVE

AN OPTICAL ILLUSION
OR PROFUSION WITH REALITY

....

*"Give me understanding and I shall observe the law, Yea, I shall observe
with my whole heart. Make me go into the path of thy commandments."*
Psalm 119:34

....

The *composite reasoning* with life is one of the conscious and
unconscious aspects of our journey. Our brain and body allow
us to procreate our intelligence with biological transience of time
and space. The complicated aspect of *motor neurons and movement
with psychosomatic union with life is brought to us with mind, body
and spirit, utilising all of Earth and her gifts through bio-chemistry.
This gift is a simple message – life itself is a miracle.*

The creative mind-set and ability of man has been a hypothesis
and *preclinical psychoanalysis* of precipitation regarding spiritual
learning and biology as one element. The deviation has occurred
through science and religion causing *oxymoron* with congruent
reasoning and aspects of *unseen* phenomena. To dispel this
misunderstanding our lives must find our reasoning and truth
with God. The messages of Earth and her gifts to us all are to find
our strength and courage with reality and to comply with the
power and trust of the Universe. Self-belief and courage is very
empowering to our health and bodily existence. *To understand*

our concurrent physiology with spiritual assignation with the Universe is the simple mathematics and logical reasoning with life and choice. To experience choice and compassion for both our individual structure and the vast expanse of magnitude and vibration is one of learning and growth.

> *"I thank you with my heart in heaven for the blessings and virtue of your teachings and my life with all of creation. Allow all Angels to bless my journey with health and prosperity, acknowledging the Holy Word and Covenants of our One."*
>
> *Elizabeth Jane Parker 2010*

Thus, through our mind-set and the power of truth and humility, our wisdom and knowledge will be forever cherished within Heavenly Realms. To bring our being and journey with God's blessings is to know that our brethren and sisters of life are all precious jewels within the Crown of God. Our acknowledgement and acceptance of instruction through Angelic Realms, *Masters of Destiny and all Holy Spirits,* take our journey into wonder and enlightenment through our humility superseding our shadow with life's teaching.

CHAPTER THIRTEEN

THE PLIGHT OF THE PHOENIX

....

"The word is a lamp at my feet, and a light to my path."
Psalm 119

....

Through *the avenues of change* and life itself, we must understand our purpose and journey with time. We are all forever seeking the knowledge and treasures of divine understanding. We are all of God's creation through eternal knowledge and virtue. However, when we are born our innocence and growth have much outer intervention and influence. Our modern world is dominated by monetary gain and material gain. Consequently we all believe in youth, impression and living life to the full! As time passes we are forever seeking ways of regeneration with biological transience and mortality. Modern life within the Western World especially expects immortality with youth and appearance. The fundamentalism of vanity supersedes the excitement of intelligence and knowledge with our World and her assets.

However, our lives do not remain the same and each passing year will bring changes to our appearance and physical structure. We will transform through life into milestones of mortality. We will become advanced in years and the assets of our youth will become a past reality. Through our experiences and format with life, however, our eternal spirit will *glean* and renew our knowledge into the realms of eternity. Through our experiences with challenge we will find a *renewed* vitality and reasoning with our God. Through our journey we will pick up the threads of reinforced quintessence through understanding our purpose and challenges with life. The backbone of our life can be strengthened with the belief that through our existence and association with Earth and her changes, we can enjoy our senior moments with time and space. We can accumulate the years of living into a momentous extravaganza of equilibrium and adventure with learning.

To truly understand the values of life and the hereafter, our belief is to know that life itself is only the beginning of our eternal body of light and journey through the Cosmos. Our belief in our fellowship with all of humanity is to know that Angelic reasoning can absolve our mistakes and sorrow in life, with the realisation that we can forgive ourselves and others for dishonour. We as humanity need to know and believe in the gift of life and the virtues we constantly seek as mortality, but to know that through our journey with life we can all find happiness at any stage and crossroad we encounter. The love of *Jesus Christ* came to show us this two thousand years ago. However, the truth has yet to be discovered by humanity and the respect of our brothers and sisters through God and his eternal love.

Our precious Planet is currently in crisis. To demean and ignore this is the sadness of not listening to the *"heavenly voice."* Through ignorance and greed we are losing the jewels and treasures of existence. To deny and ignore this has been the way of many through the millennia of past endeavours. The New Age of reality and reasoning is about to begin with Heaven.

Heaven must be brought to us all now and for future generations and sustainability of life and existence with Earth. Sceptics there are, but they must dissolve their doubt and critical denial with the challenges we now face.

Hope and glory are achievable for all of mankind, but the current millennium has brought doubt to belief. To follow our star *The Earth* is one of reality and reasoning through spiritual assignation with biology. We as humanity have simply *"lost our way"* and defy the beauty and transition we undertake with life and reasoning. We need to know about hope and glory bringing the love of all religions, politics and assignation with time into divine intelligence with mind, body and spirit rectifying the mistakes of history and our current existence with life.

CHAPTER FOURTEEN

PRELATE DIGNITARY AND
STARLIGHT INNOVATION

....

"Thy testimonies are wonderful: therefore doth my soul keep them."
Psalm 119

....

The *intelligence and creativity of man* has yet to unite and prosper upon the *Earth Plane*. The unification of virtue and truth is superseded by desire, lust, and greed and ego invention with reasoning our reality. The truth and vibration of belief has yet to be adorned upon the head of human vanity and denial. Through the avenues of disrespect our humanitarian prosperity has ontologically dismantled our World of Nature. Despite generations bringing the reality of this many people believe all will be well through their individual karmic transference respecting the assets of our Planet.

However, we must all acknowledge that we are connected with biology and the mathematical accumulation and reverberation of existence. The reality and reasoning of life is to share and procreate our assets with Earth. Through the elevation of our natural intelligence we must realise that we are destroying the very essence of our being through *Universal Ignorance* upon the Earth and her sphere. Through the passage of our Earth and her journey with time, mankind has *overridden* the beauty of life and to believe in virtue over adversity. Our current status within the *Universe* is yet to be known and through the intervention of Divine Understanding can we all begin to accumulate our brotherhood and sisterhood of evolution and life itself.

The salvation of our World now depends upon the good overriding the bad knowledge associated with monetary gain and personal prosperity. Through the minefield of sceptics, aversion, denial, cynical and diverse disassociation our greater powers within the realms of reality and reasoning must now be heard. As a result of the truth and sadness of our current dilemmas as both natural and supernatural beings, immanent messages will now be heard through the channels of purity and light, through illustrative virtuous, intent and belief.

"The love of God is in us all when we seek without vengeances and hate. The love of God is always virtue and the treasures of knowledge that abides with love and honour."

CHAPTER FIFTEEN

OUR FEET UPON EARTH AND SALVATION OF HEAVEN

....

*"Keep thy foot when thou go to the house of God,
and be more ready to hear."*

Eccl 5

....

To *shape our lives with virtue* always bring us to the question of humility and honour. However, truth is the greatest virtue in life and to understand this we must all realise our conscious reasoning and our intuitive unconscious amalgamating with humble origins. To speak, know and be our truth with the seven sacraments of virtue is simply to understand our mortal fibre with our moral fibre converging into one aspect of our learning with God, that learning is based upon humility and honour to all people.

Through our past millennia and all previous footsteps with mankind, we have all overlooked our perspicuous intentions with virtue. Understanding our coalescing quintessence has been blinded by influence, dogma and authoritarian tyranny regarding our individuality and format with *Earth Nirvana and God*. So, through the time and space of reasoning we as humanity have built a crenelated *Bastian* with fellowship and truth. Thus, our worldwide understanding is *"grounded"* with misunderstood ramification with God and all followers of religion, politics and authoritarian dilemma. How did this happen?

Endemic endurance has been the necessity through history to conceal different sects and belief with religion. The followings of truth have been denied and the shadow aspects of creation have violated the patristic writings and beauty of God and his Angels, together with Mother Earth and her foundation with life. The planetary evolution with biology and life itself has become one or ignorance. That God created the Heavens and Earth is considered a myth. Supposition through study and science attempt to disprove and ignores Angelic and Heavenly construction. This erroneous aspect of accumulating and respecting diversity is the plangent dishonour and unreceptive reasoning of many sceptics with the miracle of life itself.

Our lessons with the gifts of life have yet to be learnt as *the whole picture* with humility and honour to all things – to appreciate and admire the gift of us all merging into one of truth and respect for our Planet and her life giving assets, to appreciate and believe in virtuous intent and respect of people who are blinded by their desires. Through the avenues and pathways chosen with malfunction may we bless them but move on and learn to grow with our Mother of Invention. Our Earth is our salvation and to bring this message is to know that our power with all things is to serve both God and our Earth for unification and truth. She brings to us the beauty and understanding of life, but to know that we are all eternal seekers with vibration and light. *To know that from every single grain of sand upon the beach of life, we belong to each other.*

CHAPTER SIXTEEN

SYSTEMS ANALYSIS AND MEDITATION ANALGISING LIFE AND REASONING

....

"To everything there is a season, and a time to every purpose under the heaven, a time to be born, a time to die."

....

A *hypothetical analogy of life* and reasoning can bring our hypothesis of modern life into anachronism with holy spiritual message – when we all assume that we are isolated with individualism and essence being apart from each other. *To assume that we simply exist within the Universe without responsibility for our Earth and our one is a misunderstanding of virtue.*

Spirituality is at one with our Earth and Nature. The realism of this is simply seen and felt by us all every day of our lives. Through sceptics and disbelief that God is part of us all we become a prisoner of conscience and a "padlock" to our quintessential understanding within the Universe. Lessons are the journey we all undertake from birth. The choices and aspirations of us all are taught to us through our parochial surroundings and relationships with each other. The benefits of our lives come to us through comfort and security of tenure. The realism of our spiritual essence is our life and passage with God and his Angelic Realms. The realism of the essence of us all is simply to find our virtues with life and live our purpose seeking knowledge and gift with the challenges of reality and reasoning our spiritual immortality with biology.

Caring and sharing cannot be expressed enough when speaking of *Divine Reasoning*. Divine reasoning and recognition through the channels of God and our Mother of life bring us all to know that heavenly blessings accumulate when we find the treasures and beauty of transcendence when we actually believe in our inner sanctum and outer sanctum being at one.

Our meditation with life is to live each day knowing and believing in our *"unseen"* parallel Universe and Heavenly blessings of the Holy Order and Realms of God. Our prayers and absolutism and knowledge grow and spread through our endeavours to continuously seek and define the message of God. Throughout our lives we can all *see* our reality but know that through the *Dimensions of our Cosmos* and the alignment with Earth, we are all beneficiaries of Gods jewels and treasures with life. Through the power of self-belief and virtue we can open many doors with joy.

CHAPTER SEVENTEEN

ANGELIC ORDINATION AND THE ELECTROMAGNETISM OF OUR SUB-CONSCIOUS

....

"All this I have proved by wisdom: I said I will be wise: but it is far from me. That which is far off, and exceeding deep, who can find it out?"
Eccles.9

....

Through *our journey with the Christ Light and God* we must all understand our origins with *Holy Order* and the Covenants of reasoning our litigation with life and heavenly source. Through many eons of change the sadness of the Angelic message has been lost and now through money and prosperity of individualism, the message of Holy Angels has become one with commercialism and profit.

However, the truth about eternal messengers is one of cosmic alignment with the evolutionary process of time and space integrating and transforming with the miracle of life and reasoning. Their vibration and healing is one of powerful atonement to both body and soul when we truly believe and trust the Universe. Through balancing the human soul with the aspirations of votary virtue, their kinetic energies transform and update *Karmic Passage* with discernment and healing.

The journey we undertake from our birth is certainly one of

challenge. The dexterity of reasoning our lives is now through modernistic translation and with spirituality becoming a *profit-making venture* with Angelic Messages and healing. Unfortunately, the magnitude of Nirvana and Nature with life is now a condescending condition with many people striving to compete with the reasoning and the objectivity of God and Mother of life. The sadness once again is that humanity is completely missing the point and the free messages given to us all through our sub-conscious, intuition and imagination, is now losing momentum, and we fail to *listen* to our truth and Holy Angels of God.

True messages of Divine Reasoning are the Way showing aspects of our lives, through Angelic Mediation and virtuous thought processes with life and spiritual assignation. The vibration of the Earth becomes one with us all when we understand the beauty of evolution and existence with our beautiful but scarred Planet. Thus, as with Angelic recycling and beauty, we all need to realise that we are not indispensible beings as matter. Through the elevation of our spirit into the realms of understanding and our virtuous passage with life, the vibration of us all can once more be attained through responsibility and respect. The honour and containment of our passage *can truly be one of reflective reasoning and rectification: through allowing our belief to conjoin with our brethren and sisters of life with Angelic systems of healing.*

Through the affirmations and realistic belief that our *Planet can be One* will be the contemplation of our *Universal Intelligence* formulating and contributing to both metaphysical transformation and biological reasoning with logic and truth. *The Natural World* is one of magnitude and a complete balance with Angelic colouration and vibration. The seniority and supreme knowledge of this aspect of evolution has yet to be understood by mankind. The beauty of transition is about us all understanding and respecting our lives and that of others – through caring and sharing our assets. As with Angelic recycling our darkness, we can all through the next millennia uplift our vibration into the realms of *Heavenly Blessings and Eternal Knowledge* – without the necessity of monetary contribution towards our Universal learning and absolve. The message of purity and light transforming our lives is to know that we are brothers and sisters of creation and *The Cosmic Transcendence* with our Mother Earth.

"Love is a great thing, yea a great and thorough good, it makes everything heavy light, and it bears evenly everything unseen. Love desires to be aloft and will not be kept back by anything low and mean. Love is circumspect, humble, and upright. Love knows no measure, but is fervent beyond measure."

The Holy Bible

The Ancient Tree

By
Elizabeth Jane Parker

The Ancient Tree stands tall and strong
The roots are deep behest so long
Of time and space and growth define
The rings of truth of Heavens divine
Changes occur with the miracle of time
Slowly, gradually expand into sublime
In the branches that spread with life
The wisdom of years
Bring strength and courage
The wisdom of years
Bring compassion and love

Nature blends with vibration and knowledge
To witness the changes of life
The Ancient Tree is a home with a heart
For life and nature to begin and start
With each and every day it reigns
The proof of being
The proof remains
This tree of beauty of the Earth
Gives to Nature
Gives rebirth
For Animals and insects to find a home
The remarkable asset of stability
The remarkable asset of biological fragility
Will remain with God

The Angels of Blessings nurture this
The Angels of blessings allow this
The Angels are this
Nature and beauty for all to see
The knowledge and wonder for all to be
Our Ancient Tree
Our Ancient Message
That life is us all, as one

OWNERSHIP NIRVANA EARTH

CHAPTER EIGHTEEN

REALITY AND REASONING
TIMESCALE

....

"Then spake Jesus again unto them, saying I am the light of the world, he that follows me shall not walk in darkness but shall have the light of life."
St. John 8

....

The *functioning and fundamentalism* of living and understanding is the origination and growth of our timescale with life. From birth through every milestone, we navigate our mind-set with ownership and individuality. In the psychoanalysis of our fears, doubts and subjective reasoning our mind-set is the self-aware factuality of our journey with life, reasoning with our wisdom to elevate our insecurities into positivism. To say that humanity is without fear and doubt is indeed an untruth. Through the avenues of life we proceed on many journeys and fail to find our destination. The psychological blocks can often confuse our status quo and equilibrium and our belief and loves become a plaint of misdirection with mind-set confusion. Blame and obscurity cause us imbalance and through a metaphysical dilemma we become lost.

Human growth is the imperceptible transition through biological transformation from birth, until our milestones reach maturity. Maturity is the goal we all seek through our incarnation and self-awareness with life. However, as spiritual beings we are all on a journey with biology. The emphasis upon us all is to believe in each other but recognise and realise we are all contributions towards God and our fellowship with all things. Our humble origins from a seed of life have grown and established the assets and sustenance of our *Mother*. Our world, the Earth, are connected both spirituality and biologically.

The Universe is us all and through fellowship and each other we can live with the remarkable assets of beauty, transforming the excursion of reasoning our reality with the strength and courage or our wisdom and compassion with change. We are all teachers and receivers. We are all gifted and born to share our knowledge without the greed and lust money brings to mankind. Money is not God, God is not money.

Through the beauty and transformations of life we are the treasure and gold of presenting our lives with the grace and serenity of Angels. We are all *part of a huge mega structure*. We are all related through Earth and her assets with life. If only we could all see this! If only we could begin to appreciate and understand each other. If only we could be honourable and respect others with love and compassion. Mankind has much to learn. Mankind has much to know. Mankind has unfulfilled the messages of his *Ancient Forebears*. Without understanding each other and respecting the diversity of Philanthropic virtues and belief, we will find our journey and understanding difficult.

Through understanding and healing ourselves individually and as one unit, we can all begin to create a better World. This, therefore, is one message for *The New Age* – that money does not rule us. Money does not bring happiness to our World and connection. Money is not reasoning our lives with virtue. Until we understand about truth, love and sharing all of our assets with each other, we must understand that our spiritual one has a long journey with darkness. To balance this is a beginning. To understand this is the trial of our lives. To know this is the belief and rectification with God and his Angels.

You as the reader must decide this truth.

CHAPTER NINETEEN

OUR ONE OWNERSHIP NIRVANA EARTH CREATIVE CREATION

....

"Be doers of the word, and not hearers only"
– Jas.i.22.

....

To *understand* a simple message is that our mind, body and spirit belong to God. Through our lives we are all ignoring the truth. Our mind belongs to all aspects of our devotion to Earth and her resources. Our intelligence and mind-set allow us all to proceed along our path of purpose with all materialism materialising into change and the realisation we are one.

How do we define with definition our one truth? How are we all associated with God through linguistics, belief, creed, race and diversity? How are we all connected and reconnected with our self-awareness as ordinary human beings? How do we fulfil our passage with our *Mother Earth* and her life-giving attributes? Again, we move forward with questions. These questions need answering by us all individually. These questions bring us to understand humility and our humble origins with life. These questions are essential for human growth and our one with all things. Our lives pivot around these questions. We are all biological growth and sustenance. Mind, body and spirit are all assets of gift and life with our Planet. So much is taken for granted in our modern world. Once again, through our passage with life we must all realise that we belong – belong to the magnitude and geographical advances with time and space. We all belong to an ever-changing spectrum through the Universe. We all belong to planetary alignments and the power of life given through magnetic fields and electro dynamisms of immense power. We all need to understand that the electricity from our mind, body and spirit emanates from a miracle of creation.

Philosophers through the ages of man have *seen* with wisdom the simple aspects of dimension and electrodynamics with time. Through our mind-set and the power of our biological fragility we can assimilate and pro-create the meaning of life with virtue.

Through the ages of this Planet she has *seen* and experienced both the termination of life force and a resurgence of birth. Through ages and changes of multiple millennia the sea has grown and much land has been lost. Through the aspect of Atlantis and the losses of civilizations and the changes occurring through natural disasters and oceanic increase, the World has developed into a *"thunderous"* vibration of malfunction and misunderstanding with natural resources – wars, hatred and downfall. From this many have decided that 2012 is the *end*. Once again, the fear and retribution of the resultant negative mind-set is the lure of *jinxed* negativity. Why?

Mankind is indeed intelligent. The brain function is electrodes and messages of minute proportions unseen by the human eye, but through dialectic and diaphanous diameter we can utilize our thoughts and positivism into attainability and growth into other millennia. As intelligent beings, have we summarised our pro-creation with realistic aspirations with timescale?

The starting block of our future prosperity with this Planet is to understand and change our intelligence into *one* of hope. Through hope our thoughts will turn eventually into a blessing of sharing and caring for each other, but appreciate and understand the sustainability of our Planet without greed, authoritarian politicians and power-abusive leaders of our Nations. The power of each and every person who believes in the humble origins of our growth into sustainable and realistic aspirations for our future is essential.

Thus: to believe in the Heaven and Earth connection we can all bring our children into the future with the strength of knowledge, believing in God and his virtues – believing and pro-creating sustainability and respect for our World of Wild life and realism with Angelic connection with all things.

Elizabeth Jane Parker 2012.

CHAPTER TWENTY

UNIVERSAL HEALING AND SCRIPTURE

....

"Let every soul be subject unto the higher powers."
Romans 13

....

The *transcendence of our spiritual unification* is to follow our Earth and her ever-changing spherical symbolism with our Universe. The syllabus of our changes throughout the heavenly vibration of us all is to understand and respect all other creeds, religions and practising love of our God. The symmetry and collaboration with life and the miracles of evolutionary phenomena is intrinsic audio frequency with our Mother, and transmogrifications and Holy Spirit unilaterally combining with Heaven. Our Earth and her mythology provide our Universal Intelligences to amalgamate into *Angelic Vibration* through the channels of purity and light. Our Universal strategy for mankind is to all eventually understand that we are on a spiritual journey with life and reasoning. And through the channels of virtuous belief and realisation we can all unite and raise the vibrations of love, light and transcendence with *our Divine Mother and God our Father.*

Phonetic voices from our Masters are for us all, to know and learn throughout the next Millennia. We must all acknowledge that our Masters do not reside upon the Earth Plane. Through ancient knowledge and philanthropy they have ascended into the realms of *Holy Scripture* and healing for our one. Their presence upon our Earth ascended into supreme teaching and thus only through purity and light will heavenly messages be given.

The inseparable truth about life is to believe in the mortal aspect of growth, sustainability, learning and representation of our God and Divine Mother with aspirations of healing our brethren and sisters with love, honour and generosity. The Universal message to us all is to dissipate and disintegrate all aspects of extreme darkness. The balancing act of us all is to find forgiveness and to relieve the power of downfall into one of understanding.

In heaven we are all united with truth, belief and love. We belong to *the Holy Spirit* and the guidance of purity and light. We belong to unification and amalgamation with intelligence, knowledge and forbearance. Angelic words are powerful to our light upon the Earth. For our Divine Mother is beautiful and her connections with Angels bring our understanding to a greater enlightenment. Our awakening with enlightenment brings us all to know that we are indeed blessed with virtuous reasoning when we use our knowledge to undermine the power of darkness over light. Darkness is the imbalance of our Earth at this present time. And before we can all unite on Earth with our Angels, we must understand that we are all special in *God's Eyes* and that our Divine Mother brings us the value of life, giving, sharing and being at one with Heaven and Earth.

O merciful Jesus, enlighten Thou me with clear, shining, inward light, and remove away darkness from the habitation of my heart.

CHAPTER TWENTY ONE

THE ESSENCE OF ELECTRODYNAMICS

....

"The Magnitude of our reasoning begins with hope and valour superseding the essence of downfall or challenge to our virtue. From this learning we can elevate our understanding with love and light teaching us to move on from disappointment. Through the elemental understanding of virtue and love we move away from all trauma and disrespect from others to our soul incarnate."

Elizabeth Jane Parker 2011

....

Enjoyment *and prestige* become poetry in motion with the sequential events we accumulate through life when we embrace our soul and spiritual assignation with time. We as humanity formulate and attribute our life towards each and every day with evincing fortitude through acknowledging our weakness with acceptance and serenity. Through our weaknesses our impermanence is recognised and evaluated with reasoning. Through reasoning *our misadventures* with life we can learn and grow with our allotted time absolving our mistakes.

Each and every person with life can utilise their mind-set promotion with determining and practising forgiveness. Forgiveness is the strength and courage to overcome our pride with love. Through our emotions with life some people find difficulty in *not letting go* of dishonour to their individualism and maintain their grounding status with *bittersweet* energies curtailing their natural immunotherapy. Through lessons and courage our lives precede around every bend we encounter with the invisibility of future predictions to imbue our visions with virtuous intent. However, the lessons of life are essential for our spiritual growth and to misunderstand our purpose will not receive the natural assets of progressive learning and absolve when we all deny our weaknesses as a *weakness*. To make sense of this is to understand our weaknesses are our learning curve. Through acknowledgement, acceptance and forgiveness we learn to find our natural footing with life. Our natural footing is to see perspective with resolving our weakness with intelligent reasoning and to perceive our fellowship with life as a *journey*. Through *ethnological hypermedia* and communication we can process our *hydroelectric biology* into the realms of example and justification to our virtue. Our hypothesis in life is to rectify reason and exonerate all transgressions and dishonour for fellowship with the movement and change of our Earth each day she moves spherically around the Sun.

The implication and intellectual reasoning of our status quo is to understand Earth and her journey through time and space with her natural electrocardiograph with ecology, transmutation with transmogrify and transoceanic votive with the Moon. Our future within the New Age is not to precipitate or foretell our future with prediction as was the old way, but through our supernatural assignation with the spirit world that have now passed into the light, we will all now utilise our natural belief and intelligence with virtuous reasoning with life.

Together as an individual we find aspirations with learning but follow our path with God with virtue. Developing with our spherical formation with his Holy Angels is indeed a wonderful journey with pragmatism and astrophysics with biological containment. The essence of this combines and integrates with our entire natural world through evolution and time with the energies of light and water combining with our nutrients with Earth. Her importance for our spiritual assignation is a gargantuan gateway into heavenly realms. Angelic intervention is the pillar from which these gates are the sentinel discernments with virtuous reasoning and the *white light of reality*. However, with choice comes ego and through the laws and challenges with ego Angels cannot recognize ill-intent with virtue.

The balance of hydroelectricity is about purity and valour formulating with the geometrics of Angelic reasoning. *Our heart is about our truth connecting with all elements of nature, love, light and being. To cherish this is to believe in the sanctity of peaceful transference with truth, honour and love. These ethological meanings are the practises our life embraces with our honour ability for all things.*

Our intelligence with life is to understand our virtues with truth. To deny our truth and weaknesses is the sadness for many. For God shines his light through us all, understanding our weaknesses and sometimes dishonour. Through our journey with life we can all overcome our sometimes misinformed judgements with fellowship. Thus, to find our passage with light and truth our adherence to Divine Law must be understood. Thus, we move into another sphere of learning.

Humanitarian Beginnings

Elizabeth Jane Parker 2011

Walk *thee in the way of our LORD*, for through the sight of love all will prosper with virtue. The sight of our GOD brings only true love when we believe in virtue and the messages of Angels. Our journey with time will teach us all about prosperity and intelligence bringing us all away from desire, need and travesty. Through the message of *Jesus Christ* he taught us all to encompass God and the teachings of his divine followers. Through the history of our passage with Earth all religions have shown this belief. The sanctification of virtue must be acknowledged.

Healing our planet is about us all. No man can deny with truth and the teachings of God through all creed and religion, when love is apparent. The sight of us all will never want with the knowledge and intelligence of *"The Christlight."* Through our adversity and sometimes downfall we can all follow "The Way" with truth, understanding and love. Thus, mankind will need to heed the word of God once more. We must all listen and hear our brethren but to know that the *Lord of Love* speaks through us all when we find our true purpose with God and Goddess of life and reasoning.

We are beginning again and our journey must begin with love and resume again with understanding. Through the elemental reasoning of divine discernment we can all appreciate the eternal knowledge once more.

We must all remain humble throughout our lives. Through the transition period we are ordinary beings. We are all micro particles of *The Universe* and at every moment we all live, we need to remind ourselves, as humanity, that we are a small part of God's plan.

That as ordinary people throughout the world we have literally grown from a seed. That seed was a mathematical assimilation with time and space. Our allotted beginnings were humble and small. We must understand that every particle of life has grown from humble beginnings. The Earth and her association with our Universe has been the evolutionary graduation through timescale and eternity. From the highest to the lowest upon the Earth, we are but a speck of dust among the multitude of stars within our galaxy and beyond.

Heavenly Father And Mother Divine

Bring me the blessings of your gift into my life
Allow me the peaceful transitions of virtuous intent
Allow me O Holy Angels of God and Love
To bring a message
To bring Divinity into spherical understanding
Heavenly Mother allow me the transcendence of your Beauty
Allow me the appreciation of your gifts
Allow me the appreciation of your love
Allow me to give without question

The honour, truth and generosity of the Universe
Allow me to understand and love all of my brothers and
sisters with life
Allow me to grow and realise throughout my life
Of all things of beauty
Of all things of change
Of all things of wisdom
Of all things of love
O Heavenly father allow me your strength and courage
Allow me to overcome all obstacles with grace
Allow me to be at one with your knowledge
Allow me to know of your beauty and life
O Heavenly parents of life and gift
Allow me to follow your stars
Allow me to follow and know, believe and realise
Your existence as one
Allow me to be in your presence and feel your love
Every day of my life

CHAPTER TWENTY TWO

THE BRAIN DRAIN OF HUMANITYS

....

*"Healing is a matter of time, but it is sometimes
A matter of opportunity."*
"Hippocrates."

....

We *must all think* during this chapter about human growth and the composition of our lives as cellular, chemical and atom functioning with life. Our body is a communication with cellular, chemical atoms, organic compounds and organic molecules. To survive with all aspects of our complicated chemistry, we rely simply upon the oxygen and sustenance of our Planet. Where would we be without them? Water is a simple and stable compound of life, where would we be without water? The basics of our human form are indeed complicated workings, but without the simplicity of *Oxygen and Water* we would not survive. How do we appreciate this as a big family of *Billions upon our Earth?* How do we acknowledge and appreciate the elements of our Planet performing and utilizing these two components through our life?

Our brain organizes and oversees our growth, and bodily functions. To study and understand the complication and marvel of electrolytes, atoms, nerve cells and our heart, lungs, liver and intestines is indeed fascinating and time consuming. However, the whole picture of our biology is an *outside* presentation. We are contained as one individual being. We have a body of miracle and use. How many people truly appreciate and understand this?

Our modern World has access with education to understand anatomy and physiology, for education and knowledge. Health Practitioners study for many years learning about our bodies. We learn to treat, heal and maintain our health with education. However, who actually researches and maintains our Planet and her health? How do we see her needs with that of our own and all of Natural Resources? As intelligent beings how have we understood the beauty of spirit and biology as one? We need to ask these questions. We need to understand and appreciate the basics of our miracle with life. We need to understand and pro-action the *saving of our Planet* as a natural mother of life. We cannot distance ourselves any longer from the truth. We as brothers and sisters of life need to care for ourselves and our brethren and sisters with the knowledge of our supernatural connection with God, our brain is used for survival and knowledge throughout our lives. What exactly do we really know about our brain and the thoughts with which we all have? Thus, to learn and appreciate the parallel Universe beyond our sight are very real, and through a small receiver within our brain and our heart we connect our astronomy with astrophysical dimensions. Do we believe this?

Through *Ancient times* mankind was not knowledgeable as we are today about medicine and health care practices. His brain utilized senses and abilities through spiritual and biological belief. The distraction of modern-day facilities such as T.V, computers, mobile phones and all other modern aspects of the 21st Century were unknown. Thus, through his and her life, audio frequency and methods of communication from our other dimensions were more realistic and easily heard.

We have lost much of our ability to *"hear"* and *"see"* our lives with realistic aspirations and intentions. Through the convenience of modern technology we no longer need to use the part of our brain and receptors that were once used by us all. We have forgotten that we simply belong to our Planet through understanding and appreciating *"the Master's Voices"* from Heaven. *For through our Masters the Angels can understand our biology and functioning with life. Through the many voices of Heaven we can all bring about the immaculate and lateral thinking of our Ancient Brethren.*

Our body and soul is indeed the vehicle we use to drive our energies through life. Our soul is indeed a messenger and receiver from Heaven. Our light can shine for each other and bring the facets and changes of our future into our intelligence *when we all realize that we are immortal beings of God. There are no endings and there are no beginnings. The Sanskrit Wheel of eternity goes around the Universe unpinning the spectrum of change with life and reasoning.*

CHAPTER TWENTY THREE

ELEMENTAL CHANGES AND HOLY COMMUNION

....

"For by one spirit we are all baptized into one body, whether we
are Jews or Gentiles, whether we bond free and have been made
to drink all into one spirit."
I Corinthians 12

....

Time – *how do we understand time?* The basics of our humanity
as one is about sharing and caring for our mother earth and her
resources. Time is the transient period of learning for every
individual upon this planet. Half measures of leniency are not
appropriate for our future with progress. We, as human beings,
need to understand about our future sustainability now. The
world as a whole needs to change. That change is not apparent
at this time. The complacency and reality of reasoning our
future is not worldwide unification but that of token pockets.
Tokens for change are few. We as humanity take for granted our
earth and her assets.

The world has grown through millennia after millennia
compounding into millions of years. The growth and
functioning of our world has predominately been balanced by

earth and her elements, earth movements, climate and catastrophes. The elements of her natural history have grown from primitive life into resultant diversity with time on her side. However, human beings have changed this. How do we as one species account for our obvious need for restoration? How do we, as intelligent beings and intrigue, possibly understand the dilemma and drastic affect we all have produced upon our earth? We still do nothing that will make a worldwide impact on our limited time to actually change and make amends.

There are so many wonderful aspects of the human race and the gifts of us all. Unfortunately, we fail to understand that spirituality and biology are both responsible for the mess we are now in. Yet still we fail to actually "see" our world is in need as one whole sphere. Our intelligence is amazing. We are amazing. However, many do not understand and fail to recognise this. We fail our world as one. We fail our natural world in abuse. We fail ourselves in using our supreme intelligence and knowledge to simply undo karmic intractable dilemma we are facing.

Oh dear! Mankind is now using up the very essence of his evolution and availability for sharing and caring about all of life and resources. The question is, *why can people of power and control not see?* The point is, we as human beings need to demystify all spiritual reasoning and understand the factual elements of heavenly blessings from God. Denial that he exists is prevalent and undiluted in our modern spectrum with life. To bring a message is now absolute. To bring a message to people so they will understand is a comeback of *Holy Communion* bringing the messages of Heaven.

Devon's Delight

Elizabeth Jane Parker
November 2010

The early morning winter sun,
Over the sea and waves become
Peaceful silence of early charm
We begin with tea and a soothing balm,
November is ending, December to begin
The lines of division bare and thin,
For cold and frost sprinkle the Earth
Showing the signs of Christmas with mirth
Our love of beauty and feeling of joy
Of early beginnings the day to enjoy

After breakfast we walk into Croyde
Bulls in the field we hope to avoid!
The grazing sheep upon frosty ground
Munching and staring without a sound
Owners and dogs running upon the hill
Over the path we walk,
Silent and still
Apart from the birds, sing their song
The brambles of summer have now long gone.
They return with decay into the ground
To building the soil, the futures surround
For summer's return after winter and spring
The building blocks of life will once more begin.
The elemental changes,
Nature brings this and rearranges.

We all understand the creation of God and his wife
Understanding the seeds and mother of life
Understanding that nature is never remiss
The evolution of living brings us this.
To understand the formation of living
With unseen atoms eternally giving

The pale blue sky and fluffy white clouds
The sapphire blue sea splashing with shrouds
Of foam and spray upon the rocks
Oyster Catchers and Gulls, integrated flocks
Rooting for food and searching the shore
Their survival essential to seek and explore

We all know that within our hearts
The timescale of life begins and restarts
Our spirit with God is a time and measure
Of seeing life's wonders is always a pleasure
That Earth is our pride
For us all to enjoy
For our future
For us
For all

The Holly red berries,
The fruits of the season
Display their wealth of the festive season.
The beach flows with running water
Down from the Hills making a path,
Running into a welcoming sea,
From clouds above eternally be.

To know the changes bring eternal persistence
Elemental restoration, continuous existence
To allow humanity to know the truth'
To allow intelligence to perceive and hear
From Holy Angels about God, Light and Love
For all
For Earth
For life

The Messengers of life return every day,
In every way,
To understand positive and negative,
Brings growth again
Our belief
Structure
Our One

The second day brings gentle snow,
Upon the scenic beauty bestow
The silvery rays from the Sun shine through
Out of specks and sky so blue
Silver and gold light, is a film of wonder
Across the sea, the horizon and yonder
Reflecting the golden shape of the Sun,
Minimal flecks of light do this
Upon the tapestry of scenic bliss

The expanse of sea brings another shore,
Across the divide of oceanic galore
For God understands the beauty of space.
In demonstration of spirit within this place

This place called Earth.
The complete wonder and beauty of The Universe
For us all to share with dreams…
For future generations and pleasure
The Heaven and Earth golden treasure

CHAPTER TWENTY FOUR

MONEY – THE MAJORITY RULE

....

"Take heed therefore unto yourselves, and to all of the flock, over which the Holy Spirit has made you overseers, to feed the Church of God, which he has purchased with his own blood."
The Acts 20

....

The *fundamental strategy of time and space is the magnitude of history ever learning and refreshing knowledge.* The Earth and her spherical journey with atoms, chemistry, elements and simple mathematical accumulation allow us all to unilaterally exist. Evolution and sporadic geographical and universal changes with time ever move empower our escapement with reality to meet balance with time itself. Essentially, philanthropic intelligence with God and our Divine Mother accumulate our understanding and age-long association with biology and chemical reconstruction. Through the timescale of reality and reasoning the necessary human strategy to recycle our assets and availability with Earth and her resources, is yet to be focused and understood. Her treasures within the universe are assimilated through eternal astrophysics and metaphysical origination from source with chemical components working with time. Thus, humanitarian intelligence must now recognize and realize the truth with sustaining our sustenance and natural resources produced through the changes of our Earth spinning through time and space.

The consequence of man and his incessant desire for materialism and money have indeed caused a worldwide mutilation of the natural elements of our Earth and her movement circumnavigating the Sun. Within our *Universe* the timescale element of history has now distorted the life force of our current generation and spherical learning spheres with heaven. Through ignorance and greed our world as humanity is slowing decreasing our attributes with time and space. Our resources are realistically running low. The ever increasing dilemma with disbelief and scepticism with life respecting all resources becomes a hypothetical crisis for our mortal existence within earth and her sphere.

Consequent changes must now be understood for our future generations and the reality of life and existence. The facets of change must now be taught and understood. Respect of our Planet and that of her natural elements and gift to us all will be numinous teachings, with power shifting the misunderstandings we are currently now experiencing.

The Earth is now changing her climate. This is a natural ramification of timescale with the galaxy. Mankind has certainly during recent times misunderstood life and the aspects of our learning about value. The valuation of the earth and her resources are currently *disinteresting* to sceptics, money makers and business. Unfortunately, the economy is value by monetary worth and the accumulation of wealth for individual glory and accumulation. Balance is not known at this particular *moment in time* within the *twenty-first century.*

If we all believe that with the increase of population and the non-availability of resources is in fact implausible then we must all understand the reality of our Earth and her sustainability. We must all understand that simply taking and not replacing will bring a plausible truth *"we lose the very essence and balance of life."* Life is indeed precious. However, this is only seen through ownership and material benefits beyond reasonable consideration and worldwide conscience. *The balance has yet to be known and understood for global understanding and futuristic prospects for us all.*

CHAPTER TWENTY FIVE

HELIOCENTRIC HELIOGRAPH

....

"Sing unto the Lord, all of the Earth."

....

Reflection, *communication and light,* how do we actually see this and understand the audio frequency and transmission of all of life through light, darkness and colour? To transmute the blessings of science and spirituality is currently one of disbelief for many. Despite their lives and the precocious aspects of their intelligence as adults and human beings, they live with life as a *vacuum* of circumstance without purpose. Many modern people believe in good but fail to understand the darkness of energies curtailing their journey with life. They believe that even though we live within a technological world that all of this *just simply came along.* To ignore the Earth and an appreciation that the world contains our lives is to ignore the messages and transmutations from God as our eternal father and giver of life and reason.

Through the aspects and ideology of viewing our world and the planets and the planets surrounding us, we all take for granted the immense possibilities and life. Through living and breathing within biology we all, each day, simply forget that we owe our lives to the Universe. Despite the teachings and fundamental learning with schools and universities, our modern purpose is about making money. We see this as the goal and benefit to our lives and that of our future. Through this aspect of misunderstanding we forget our purpose and journey with time and learning. We forget that we are all precious and that money constitutes a minor of part of our journey with life. We forget to honour and creatively understand the evil that money brings when we fail to listen, perceive and love our life and journey with this marvellous planet and her gifts to us all. We just simply forget and ignore the wonder and learning with life.

Thus we ask, is the story for us all? Our one journey at this moment is big business! Stocks and shares, making profit and living with greed is the order of the day. Spirituality and current modern-day thinking is that "we must earn a living" and often charge large amounts of money to give impurity a gain. They believe that the aspects of survival deny their skills and attribution and believe in making money from vulnerability and distress of purpose. The *tabernacle* of belief has now become the worship of money and material gain. The truth is, how do we appreciate our world and her assets through modernism and the purpose of grandeur and superior misrepresentation of divine message? God will serve all of his children through simple messages. Through his divine heart he will forgive us all when we understand about humility, love and sharing with all of fellowship and with all of life.

Through our journey with life, we will meet many challenges to our light and through our wisdom and courage we can all find our purpose with forgiveness and love. The true power of Angelic Messages to us all is about giving and sharing our love with the messages of God overcoming the darkness and modern disbelief in virtue.

Our God brings energies and light beyond the comprehension of many. Through the avenues and journey of living, modern man has learnt to hate, deny and debauch the love of our one. Through misunderstanding darkness and light we all lose our monochromatic balance with wisdom. Thus, our God will forgive us all when we honour him and his heart with self-forgiveness and forgiveness for all fellowship with life. Thus, the vibration and aspect of living becomes one with God and his messages.

CHAPTER TWENTY SIX

MEMORIES OF TIME

....

Life passes us all as a memory, that memory serves us all with virtue.
Virtue brings all to understand reasoning and wisdom through the
challenges that are beset us all. Thus, we learn about mortality and the
immortality of light.

Elizabeth Jane Parker 2011

....

Through *our journey* we all find challenge to our belief with God
and our Holy Mother. Through the aspirations of desire and
"betterment" we are all apt to *"run before we can walk"* with the
avenues of time and space. Through the many shadow
advances to our status quo we can all fall into a dark place,
whereby fear utilizes our light against the sacraments of
heavenly blessings. Thus, to learn about reality with spiritual
perfection we all misunderstand the messages from God. God
sends us all love every day. However, when we lose our belief
in other matters of discernment our ordinary living is unable to
escape the darkness of greed. Thus, mankind seeks to *"update"*
his technology with reasoning his desires and *"one-upmanship"*
with his allotted time. Christmas has now been lost through
desire. Ego transgresses all sacraments of virtue at the festive
season with life.

Our children are our future upon Earth, thus to teach them about the message of Christmas is about love, giving and receiving with gratitude and honour.

"Blessed be God, even the father of our Lord Jesus Christ, the Father of Mercies, and the God of all comfort, who comforts our tribulation, that we may be able to comfort them which are troubled, wherewith we are ourselves are comforted by God" – From The Holy Bible.

Life is about giving, receiving and sharing the assets of our Earth. Through the twenty-first century we all need to update our belief before our technology. The appreciation of gifts and universal message is about our lives with each other and that of our earth. To find the miracles of spirit and that with modern-day reasoning is yet to be recognised and realised through our technological age. The marvel of invention is indeed the wonder of the human brain, however, again the message to us all is indeed that the fragility of mechanical workings does not balance with the balance of universal change. Our planet has become one of *"throw away grandiose elimination."* Our thought processes and connection divert us all away from our appreciation and the divine messages of light. We all need to simply take time to learn again about appreciation and thankfulness about the material element of our being with life. We all need to ask about the festive message to all of mankind. Despite our religions and creed, the message of God to us all is about love and gratitude.

Our children need to follow us all. We need to once more teach them about the joy of giving gifts. These gifts are not about materialism, these gifts are about love, honour and truth. Acknowledgement for the *gift of life* and the choices we have.

Our lives are for many reasons. The reasons become apparent to us all eventually through our life but finding the treasures of learning and aspiration is about our containment within the confines of biology. Through our biology our spiritual enlightenment brings us into a better place when we simply learn to appreciate all of the love we contain. Love is an eternal memory and that memory will "outlive" all of our transgressions when we simply "see" our brothers and sisters with honour, truth and devotion. Thus, the divine message will reach us all through the sacramental covenants from God.

CHAPTER
TWENTY SEVEN

THE VANGUARD OF OPTIMISM

....

"Optimism and hope bring our belief into the intellectual forum for all of mankind. To trust all messages from the Holy Word of God, allows us all to grow systematically with our allotted time with space and our journey around the sun."

Elizabeth Jane Parker 2011

....

The *change of universal knowledge condenses our light into transmigration when we formulate* our reasoning upon the chakra steps. The transceiver and transcendental passing of our soul integrates with all bodies of light, when we utilize and understand transmogrify with God and his word. Thus, when we all believe and understand Holy Spirit then this brings science with transfiguration and transformation into the realms of Seraph trajectory sequence and eternal knowledge. We all work with our individual sensitization with virtue and the Holy Covenants with heavenly source. Thus our soul becomes one with all knowledge, simply and extricable when we release our ego. The semi-conductor and musicality with semibreve octaves bring Heaven and Earth into one codex with messages from God and all of his previous devotees within heavenly

107

realms. The quadrilateral emphasis of strength, courage, wisdom and compassion is the foundation of knowledge and belief for which all Angelic messages is given. The coaxial with earth and her sphere brings Angels aegis into our being and we aesthetically integrate our reasoning and actuality with earth and the universe as one element.

However, the sadness of our modern world brings many intellectuals and people who study the fact finding structure of existence, to disbelieve about God. Through their academia and intrinsic studies they are apt to vituperate the findings and ancient knowledge of creation. Thus, often materialism and disbelief presents itself to our modern world as one of compound structural learning and education for our children. The emphasis here is to bring about free thinking and for our societies to appreciate the validity of all virtuous message with life and reasoning. Life will bring many contradictions to our belief, but however through understanding the modern mind-set with ancient philosophy is to bring diversity and choice with our belief.

Our soul is eternally seeking expansion with all elements of reincarnation and knowledge accumulating with reasoning. Our lives bring divine messages and knowledge with God when we integrate our learning with virtue. The purity of our faith with life is important for *our soul's progression upon the celestial passage with time.*

Before finding our journey with optimism and belief with hope, our intellectuality as a species must now encompass respect and honour to all people and their creed, knowledge and belief. God speaks to us all through his followers. These followers indeed all speak with truth, knowledge and the fundamental reasoning with divinity and the universe. Thus to understand God's messages we all need to love and honour our brethren. To know and realise that our message is divine when we understand about our truth. Our truth is to know and believe in our eternal soul as a wonderful connection and reconnection with life and the eternal perception of the learning eye. The great spirit of our earth is about the wonders and beauty of understanding about our eternal journey with God but to live an impermanent momentum with life.

Many people have theory about our soul's originality. However, only we, as an individual hold the answers and the questions regarding our ownership and journey with life and time. Thus, this is where influence is disallowed by our belief in our individual truth and karmic passage. Only we as individuals have the responsibility to bring our life back into alignment with the chakra steps. As individual we are all responsible for the connecting with God and his reasoning. Faith and enlightenment are the treasures that maintain our originality through life. Thus, we learn about dishonour and forgiveness from our brethren. Through forgiveness and transition we will learn that we heal ourselves and others, bringing our light into our soul for eternal redemption and God.

CHAPTER TWENTY EIGHT

THE OBSCURE OBSERVATION AND OPPORTUNITY

....

The fundamental reasoning of "sight" and learning becomes plangent within heavenly spheres when we all understand our reasoning and wisdom with the gift of life and honour to all things.

Elizabeth Jane Parker 2011

....

The *Laws of Attraction* for heavenly source is indeed a gift to us all from God our Father. Through understanding his creation and love for Mother Earth has indeed been misunderstood through belligerent messages of "who is right and who is wrong." Again, modernism misinterprets God's messages about exactly "whose side God is on." We covered this aspect through "*Voices from Heaven.*" The truth about God is simply and wholly one of honour, truth and respect for our *World of One* and unification with the learning spheres of evolution and time.

Divine Law is about affinity with infinity. Divine Law is about honour, humility and life as a proactive intelligent species. Divine Law is about observation, learning and absolve for natural law and the obscurity of heavenly source teaching us all about individualism and the creed of reasoning our love for

God.   Belief is the attribute of love, honour and truth formulating and absolving our transgressions and burdens with life. Thus, the foundation of strength, wisdom, courage and compassion allows us all to learn about God and his reasoning, together with our biological mother, yes, Earth.   Earth brings many challenges as we have already discussed but to appreciate her message is one of beauty when we all believe in the Heaven and Earth symbolism with life. For, life brings many gifts to our eternal soul, thus learning with our foothold with life is the reality and reasoning with God our Father.

We all begin our lives truly, when we learn to honour, respect and love ourselves together with all of our brethren and sisters of life. Through this message, we will now begin to bring the word of God to all.   Through the strength of our heart connecting and reconnecting with heaven we will all commence again the strong belief about divinity and God's blessings to his children and their children.

Biological Transformation With God

The *human heartbeat is the vibration of all reconnection with heavenly source.   The micro particles of evolution have progressed and transmuted throughout the voluminous magnitude of spin, retrograde and direction of our galaxy. The essence of spirituality has brought gradual Angelic intervention through magnetism with Earth and her gravitational pull. Understanding our intelligences is with virtuous migration and travel through the Universe collating purity and light of the human sphere of learning together with metaphysical expansion with time accumulation. The miracle of time and transformation together with virtuous messages and learning spheres has co-ordinated the truth and validity of human essence within Earth and her vibrations. Our Masters of the Universe has attracted Angelic reasoning through their vibrations and mathematical unification with energy transforming with colour and light. Through pragmatic astrophysics and the transition of micro-organisms through history and timescale, our world of one has culminated hydro dynamics and biological components imperceptibly transforming through a "hidden veil" of light and colour. This light is produced organically with our atoms, cells and colour permeating through our chakra system of "invisible" attunement and balance with nutrients and energising properties through electromagnetism with life.*

The Earth provides these nutrients and her assets with biology transform each and every aspect of our lives with time and space with reality and reasoning our truth. The purity of our virtues with love and light are the aspiration of us all as spiritual beings with God. To understand and learn bring us all to utilize our knowledge with God and his Angelic forces. We all need to learn and understand our limited passage with life and reason in order for us all to commence upon the chakra steps and the reality of heavenly source. Through the migration of life we can all find God and the truth about our chemistry and biological foothold temporarily teaching us to accept and to learn with strength, courage, wisdom and compassion formulating our truth with life. To honour and absolve our mistakes and that of others is indeed the message of Seraph Angels and God. Through our Masters teaching us all, we can gain a better prospective and wisdom reasoning our lives.

Thus to "cherish the challenge" is to gain the power of connection with our supreme source of knowledge. Through this accumulation we can all begin to understand the reality of our existence as mankind. Through understanding and believing our universal connections and healing processes, we can change our Earth into one of immense structural renaissance with God and his teachings. Through understanding that through humility we own our lives as individuals but through the passage of learning, we can become one with our God in Heaven until we return to heavenly spheres. There are no endings within the universal structure with eternity. Thus as the saying goes, "What goes around, comes around." Through this lesson we can then understanding our immortality and mortality with life and existence.

Elizabeth Jane Parker 2011

CHAPTER TWENTY NINE

THE UNIVERSAL STUDENT MANKIND

....

*The Ancient Prophesies for Mankind are our inheritance for the future.
All lessons of absolve and manifestations of Holy Spirit through pure
channels must now be strictly adhered to. Our future is balanced by our
virtues with God and his teachings.*

Elizabeth Jane Parker 2011

....

The *propitious and prolix teachings* about truth are now a
necessary advancement for our non-observances as an
intelligent species of evolution and time. The truth and works
of our brotherhood in heaven can only teach us all when we
experience admittance of philanthropic weakness for our
individualism and our expansion as human beings.

The expansion of our intelligence is about the prologue of
God's word understanding the weakness and absolves of our
evolutionary *stadium of mishaps* regarding the journey of
mankind. We are all embarking upon God's Service when we
all appreciate and understand the workings of divine
discernment and the heavenly blessings we are all born with.

Many children in the modernistic lifestyle now believe that all possessions are the secret of their success with life. In this aspect of our future thoughts, modern day history is still *universally primitive* as intelligence diversifies into malpractice and misunderstandings about God. The true message of *Christmas and the New Year* becomes one of desire. This desire does not recognize the perspective and sight of sharing and caring. The world of our one is about change and the love we all need to share. Christmas is about giving, love and meaning. Thus, unfortunately, to receive and desire bigger and better materialism becomes our impermanent misrepresentation of this equinox of change.

Only through *free healing* can we all ascend into our truth and the love of Christ. The messages to our children should be about giving and receiving the feeling of fellowship and our world of deprived peoples. There is no answer at present to all those people who disbelieve that our questions and answers bring heaven to us all. Thus, messages must be heard for us all to begin again and understand that Christmas is about us all changing the world for those less fortunate. The true meaning of God is about us all finding the beauty of living and giving for our brothers and sisters in life.

The true meaning of celebration is about spiritual unity and love for us all. Our brotherhood and sisterhood of life is about our origins with virtue. The ancient messages to us all must once again be resurrected and understood by all. Through our next venture the circumference of learning will begin with these messages.

Eternal Embodiment

We are all God's children *through the allotropic embodiment both on earth and in heaven. The metamorphisms with life bring our soul into connection with heavenly source when we learn to understand the true messages of hierarchal learning and humility. The grounding aspect of this allows the angelic forces to perform their healing and connection with heaven:*

Before Christ our Lord ancient forbears believed in the sanctification of our holy father and his "Seraph Angels." The purity of message became lost and thus God sent his son to redeem and honour humanity. This honour was about love, truth and wisdom honouring all other religions and creed. This love was the embodiment of the "cloak of understanding" our lives and that of heavenly expansion. Only through the loving messages of all creeds and religions can we pass our divinity in the realms of life and learning as one species. Thus, we as human beings must understand our ancient fathers and the messages once given to us all.

Our journey with earth is but a minute aspect of our "Great Being" in heaven and through understanding our gift to the earth is about love and honour to all things mortal and immortal. Eventually, through the next millennia we can bring Heaven unto Earth with reasoning and love. To seek and find the treasures that lie within us all will begin to transform our vibrations and elevate this into complete love and trust with the Universe. Man created evil for his desire and greed and to speak this truth is about understanding that we can all change and bring the good of all back into the realms of divine discernment and life itself. The blessings of God are found with us all through recognizing and understanding our weaknesses. Through our admittance and belief we can all transcend our spiritual one into a better world. Thus, may God may bless you all who seek to find our parallel universe that exists only with complete love and trust for God and the creation of all things.

Elizabeth Jane Parker 2011

THE ASYMMETRICAL MULTILANGUAGE WITH METABOLISES AND SPIRITUAL ASSIGNATION

....

Part Two

....

The Sight of Reasoning
Divine Discernment

The *advancement of progress and change within the confines of mortality bring us to learn and understand the changes of individualism. The metamorphosis through "milestone" and direction are the perceptions we simply choose to "see" and acknowledge. Our biological being has "directives" and mathematical assimilation with timescale. This timescale imperceptibly moves with our planet and her evolutionary movements around the sun. Thus, our implement of existence brings our learning and teaching within "the stadium of life" and the opportunities and learning we all live through. The truth about our lives will be obvious to us all through everyday volition of our actions, thoughts and progress. This simple explanation brings us to know that our lives are impermanent with timescale and the assimilation with this fact enables us all to realise that we have "limitations."*

This is where we experience and acknowledge our truth with all things existing and growing through earth and her movements within our galaxy. She derives many of her assets with connection and reconnection with electrodynamism and movement. The portrayal again, of this simplistic explanation is to understand the forces that control us all. We have covered this aspect and now move forward again through the motive power of knowledge and learning.

The polymath of us all as mankind is the scholastic schedule with reality and reasoning our journey both biologically, scientifically and spiritually with astrophysics and asymmetrical symbolisms. The geometrical transition of us all through the power of Seraph and Archangels is about our pure energies releasing the downturn and darkness we are all apt to experience. Through the learning materialism of life, we begin to understand our individual intellect and that of our forefathers and creation. For "The Universe" is the unimaginable "spotlight" of visibility of timescale and mechanism of our journey through life. Unfortunately, sceptics and science requires the factual element of change but misunderstand the celestial recordings of our metaphysics and timescale combining with eternal knowledge and truth. Our journey incorporates many revelations and learning, the beauty and transition of this becomes apparent and transcendental with God when we all adhere to the natural reasoning we were born with, thus, the next venture will bring us all to study and learn the messages given to us all through ancient forebears. This will bring our understanding completely up to date with reasoning our reality with life and God.

For many, it is a mystery to know that we are all beautiful and spiritual sanctification when we learn to change from darkness back into light. The sadness of humanity during this day and age of the twenty-first century many people are unable to grow with timescale. The darkness formation surrounding dogma and misunderstanding denies their truth and love with God.

The "see" of life is to look, feel and know about reasoning and the transformational journey we are all upon. To actually believe is the hardest lesson for us all. Thus, our journey will begin again. Our one truth upon this earth is to learn, observe and proactively make changes to our equilibrium. Thus, the balance is universally brought to us all through our lives. The sadness of many is that they cannot and will not see this. Obstinate obscurity is preferential to change and new beginnings. This is the meaning of stagnation without virtue.

Mankind needs to understand that virtue can resurrect every day through the power of love, honour and truth. The foundation of strength, courage, wisdom and compassion will surround our aura, chakras and belief when we encompass God and his followers of celestial wonder and recognition.

Thus, our journey begins.

CHAPTER THIRTY

SOMATIC TRANSFERENCE
WITH BIOLOGY

....

"The solvency with calculus is to rectify our mistakes and the misunderstandings brought to our challenges through ego. Ego is to be understood and released through the channels of purity and light."

Elizabeth Jane Parker 2011

....

Mind, *body and spirit* perform a journey through the realms of life and reasoning. We have discovered many objectives and transferences through our mind-set promotion within the space travel and evolution with time.

Our impermanent journey with biology is indeed a limitation for our up to date progress with *universal intelligence*. This is our truth with the metamorphic reality with time. Through everyday changes and challenges we are ever seeking contentment for our intelligence and aspirations within our time slot. Through this realism with science and reasoning scepticism was born for mankind. The belief and wonder of our Universe becomes one of *diametric dissolution* for our belief and future. Thus, many scientists need factual proof and revelation with research and chemical transformation through atomic theory, in gathering evidence for us all to know and believe. Of course, again, many scientists find their reasoning and findings differ from other researchers of both mathematical and geometric reasoning's. Circumstantial eclipses may bring differences of opinion and findings. How do we actually see this as learning and maintaining our current intelligence throughout the world of diverse opinion?

Our Universe is determined by factual transformation and transfiguration through imperceptive energies through space. This simple explanation is based upon relativity and mathematical combinations. However, from this our teachings with all people must involve reasoning spiritual science with that of modern day mind-set. There have been through our histories many changes of perception. The metaphysics of change incorporate a body of balance and fragility. The behavioural science of humanity has been a *scrimmage* of misconceptions regarding who is right and who is wrong. "The *Scylla and Charybdis*" from Greek mythology brings an asymmetrical reasoning to heavenly isomorphic with God. The natural law of our physics and relationship with Earth is one of miracle with instrumental atoms circulating and providing our evolution and matter. Part of our growing intellect is to understand that our shape, form and construction with science have yet to be understood and appreciated by mankind through the world. To learn and appreciate our humble beginnings and the growth through sustenance and the life giving forces of oxygen with hydrosphere, we exist with this simplistic knowledge.

We then use our intelligence to appreciate the existence of all matter and life contained with this truth. Our oceans and purity with Earth have given us our entire bodily vehicle through the exactitude of water and plant life which formulate every foundation of life upon Earth. How do we, as individuals acknowledge and understand the existence of this very fact and truth regarding our individual life upon Earth? How do we, as individuals marvel and wonder every of our lives about this truth? From this we can begin to change our scepticism and begin to learn about our lives and the gifts that we all exist with. Why is it necessary to teach this once more to mankind? The truth is we as intelligent beings overlook our resources with Earth. We have forgotten through every millennium to simply learn to live with respect, honour and truth with our assets.

Our body has grown from biology and coerces with life and reasoning. The impermanent passing of every day, month and year are to be savoured by us all. The philanthropic virtues of our heavenly bodies and reality with eternity must now be seen and understood for our future upon Earth. Our Earth exists for us all to share, understand and sustain. Our Earth gives us all life and existence and so we need to save and preserve our wildlife, rivers, oceans, land and our lives and all balances with nature itself. Are we in fact scientifically all missing the point of humanities existence and life itself in truth. Again, you as the reader must decide.

CHAPTER
THIRTY ONE

THE SYMMETRY OF SYMBOLISM

....

"Be therefore followers of God, as dear children, walk with love."
Eph. 5

....

We *are all of God's children.* We have grown from a simple seed through the impassive transformations of biology and our natural universal intelligence with life. Understanding the strength and courage of belief is to realise the reality that our immortal soul connects with the hydrology and natural hydropathical components. The *hydrodynamics of reasoning* are the harbingers of connection with natural light through the electrodynamics of actuality and existence. Through the crystal clear elements of pure water and our biology, we are able to live and understand the symbolisms with our isosceles with geometrics. Our spiritual assignation with God makes headway into the future of reality with Earth and her essences and life giving attributes for progress and our future.

Water is indeed a great healer for us all to appreciate with realization that this component is necessary for all transformations and realities with life itself. The functioning of water as we learn is the giver of life with hydrology working with material components and micro-organisms. The emphasis upon this fact is the truth of evolution. Water gives life. Our planet Earth as we currently know is unique within our *Solar System*. Through elemental construction the volatilization of vapour from our oceans and the alignment of our Moon and Sun cause hydrosphere to form hydrostatic compounds. These compounds collectively cause rain clouds. As we know these clouds bring life. Through this simplistic knowledge we all take this for granted during our modern world.

In this fact and knowledge throughout the world we know that water is a treasure. This treasure together with *The Universe* is about us all. We are all about bio diversity and the treasure of life connecting us all. So from this small point how do we see our lives with belief and the transitions we all undertake with growth and belief from our small seed of life?

The Holy Bible

Proverbs 27 and 28

Boast not thyself of tomorrow,
For thou knows not what the day may bring forth
Let another man praise thee, and not thy mouth.
A stranger and not thy own lips
A stone is heavy, and the sand weighty,
But a fool's wrath is heavier than both.
Wrath is cruel, and anger outrageous,
But who is able to stand before envy?
Open rebuke is better
Than secret love
Faithful are the wounds of a friend,
But the kisses of the enemy are deceitful.
The full soul loathes a honeycomb,
But to the hungry soul every bitter thing is sweet.
As a bird wanders from her nest
So is a man that wanders from his place,
Ointment and perfume rejoice the heart,
So doth the sweetness of a man's friend by hearty counsel.
Thine own friend and thy father's friend forsake not,
Neither goes into thy brother's house on the day of calamity:
For better is a neighbour that is near than a brother
Far off

My children be wise and make my heart glad,
That I may answer him that reproaches me
A prudent man foresees evil and hides himself

But the simple pass on and are punished
Take his garment that is surety for a stranger
And take a pledge of him from a strange woman.
He that blesses his friend with a loud voice, rising early
In the morning,
It shall be counted a curse to him
A continual dropping in a very rainy day
And contentious women are alike
Who so ever hides her hides the wind,
And the ointment of the right hand betrays itself
Iron sharpens iron
So the man sharpens the countenance of his friend
Whoever keeps the fig tree shall eat the fruit itself.
So he that waited on his master shall be honoured.
As in water, faces answers to face
So the heart of man to man
Hell and destruction are never full.
So the eyes of a man never satisfied.
As the fining pot of silver, and the furnace for gold,
So is a man to his praise.
Though thou shall bray a fool in the mortar amount the
Wheat with a pestle,
Yet will not his foolishness depart from him.

CHAPTER
THIRTY TWO

THE LOSSES OF CONTEMPTUOUS
REASONING

....

*"We build our house upon strong foundations, strength, courage, wisdom
and compassion and work in unison for all building blocks for salvation.
Within and without the house of God is built upon integrity with love
and wisdom. The reasoning of virtue absolves our foundation with
strength through the learning spheres of virtue. Lose not thy faith with
anger. Lose not thy salvation with retribution. Teaching ourselves with
solidity and true purpose allows our reckoning to grow and expand
through love conquering all."*

Robert Grosseteste Medieval Bishop of Lincoln

....

God *is love. God is truth. God is us all when we learn to "turn the
other cheek,"* but to speak our truth with virtuous reasoning.
Through the dishonour of our brethren we learn to absolve our
love for all things, when we simply forgo anger with love and
honour stabilizing humility and knowledge. We have discussed
we are all teachers and learning with life, but the test for us all
is to appreciate opinion without *allowing* authoritarian
perplexity from our brethren who may be falling into the
darkness of obscurity. God finds us all through understanding

our purpose with humanity and the philanthropic truth of our foundation and workings with life. The temple of our *Lord Jesus Christ* was built upon the structure of understanding humility, wisdom and virtue. The temple of truth is us all, when we supersede the insubordination of darkness over light. Through the avenues of our spiritual one with all things is to love our brethren but to move away from dishonour and *isolated* reasoning with love.

As with our LORD he was persecuted and attempts were contrived to humiliate his nascent passage with God and the teachings from heaven. However, through his belief and eternal knowledge he regained his heavenly ascension through the purity of his building blocks with life.

It a sadness throughout history many people with knowledge attempt to bring their belief into dictatorial reasoning through self-righteous overtures with divine workings and message. This is our learning and passage with shadow and light to overcome influence with love and respect. The monochromatic synchronization is to honour with wisdom and reasoning of love. Through love we can utilize the power of *Angels through the Law of Attraction* with virtuous intent. Our spiritual life can grow again from the destructive elements of dishonour, through forgiveness and the piteous guilt of the house of our brethren, whomever, falling into disrepair.

Through the malfunction of darkness, many of our brethren will seek but only find bars across their path. Turning back is about faith overcoming blindness against the light. The startling effects of light can burn and destroy foundations when mankind builds his fortress against God. Only through the love of reasoning can any man or woman find the true treasures of life throughout their journey, when finding their truth and purpose with eternal knowledge and the blessings of fascination and joy about God and his true message to us all.

The truth and love of God is about forgiveness with strength and the courage to move on with our purpose without looking back. From our lessons with virtue we can find our light with all things in life. Our days through time can be a valued aspect of knowledge and expansion.

The Ultrahigh Votary With God and His Angels

Elizabeth Jane Parker

The *monochromatic radiation with healing often brings a "healing crisis" for mankind. The vitriol magnetism with darkness is brought to individualism through life and choice, when we all fail to achieve God's truth and message with life. The path of mankind was "set in stone" upon the steps of evolution. Failure to comply with our individual truth and that with God, brings all men and women to misunderstand their light. Through the darkness our soul cannot understand the distressing messages from shadow. The simple aspects of self-belief and virtue with fellowship are about understanding our light with God and Goddess with life's continuous lessons within the seven sacraments of virtue. We are all on God's mission with love on our side. Through "seeing" this aspect of our understanding the healing of our planet can commence for us all to know and believe in.*

The darkness of evil will attempt to vitiate all knowledge of beauty and transition. Mankind has yet to understand his individual responsibility with God and the messages of beauty and love upon our Earth as well as in Heaven.

The betrayal of darkness brings the anger and disappointment to our world when we fail to forgive with truth and our heart with love.

True love upon Earth is about change and the keys to heavenly blessings. Thus, understanding our love and strength with Seraph Angels is to know that our hierarchal being is calling to us all within the wilderness of life and the karmic transition we walk with.

Many bring messages of hope but fail to understand that money does not "buy our way into heaven!" True spiritual healing is brought to us all through understanding our journey through life with God and Goddess of truth. The absolutisms with humanity understanding and absolving the tyranny of evil, is to know and learn about divine message. For we all belong to God. God is not monetary gain. God is not about superiority. God is not about healing for personal gain. God is not about dishonour.

Divinity and love is about truth, belief and honour among all men and women of virtue. Virtue is the power of light and cannot be sought through career and money buying this. The truth of God is about sharing and caring about our brothers and sisters but teaching the word without expectation of gain. For the gain of our beautiful truth is about the treasures of life brought with natural intelligence and acceptance of God's love.

CHAPTER THIRTY THREE

FOR THE LOVE OF GOD

....

"The transcendence of virtue brings our vibration to the highest level of understanding when we believe in honouring our brethren with compassion. Despite all ill-will among the darkest places of humanity, we learn to understand the beauty of God through his forgiveness and love for us all."

Elizabeth Jane Parker 2012

....

To *understand the messenger* and all beings of divinity, is to know that we are truly loved. Throughout the ages of man, many people have found their salvation and understanding of God through the avenues of darkness being dissipated. Through forgiveness of all others and their sins is about understanding our own imperfection and that of our brethren. Opinion often brings dishonour when ownership becomes ignorant of love. Therefore, divinity does not judge the person for they truly judge themselves. Thus, the unhappiness of their situation is to manifest as anger and retribution towards others. A truly contented and happy person is about love and belief transcending the downturns of life and reasoning.

The messages of all religions have been lost through time and space with evolution and love. Our modern world grows darker with contempt. Thus, to teach about love over adversity is paramount for our future and the inspiration we all seek from our brethren and sisters. The power of Angels is about *The Law of Attraction* within the *Covenants of Heaven*. Thus, to attract Angelic reasoning is through us believing and understanding the crisis of life will be overcome through our wisdom and compassion. Divinity is our passage through life. We all need to know this and bring about proactively using our knowledge for each other. Love is indeed the power we all seek. However, this power cannot be abused and thus, through the seven sacraments we all can live with hope, love and honour each day of our lives.

To fall into the *Chasm of Insecurity* is when we all fail to believe the lessons of our lives. To cherish our challenge is about life's ups and downs. Some people have more than others but through this they can simply find their light again by honouring and absolve with our brethren and our planet.

Our journey with life is a wonder when we all seek knowledge and truth. The knowledge and the diversity of us all as philanthropic beings are about our God and his eternal love. The messengers from heaven will bring us all the truth and divine discernment we must all learn through the next millennia.

The Earth will continue her journey with all of the elemental changes of times past and future. She has followed this path for many millennia and timescale. However, we are all joined together with her essence and history throughout time. Thus, the wisdom of us all is now to make the changes required to raise the vibration of love and truth for spiritual assignation and life.

CHAPTER THIRTY FOUR

THE HAGIOLOGY OF LEGEND AND TRUTH

....

"Even from the days of your fathers ye are gone away from mine ordinances, and have not kept them. Return unto me, and I will return unto you, says the LORD of hosts."

Malachi 4

....

The *writings and beautiful* messages to us all have indeed been passed through ancient spiritual radiophonic medium throughout the ages of man and scripture. The quintessence of truth and reason is essential information for us all to follow and learn.

Mankind is reaching out for love but modern-day mediums seek sensationalism together with precocious messages of materialism and glamour. This attractive aspect of beauty is, however, skin deep in misrepresentation for Holy Message. Many Saints and providers of virtue were ordinary people with whom their beauty of spirit overcame the plenipotentiary influences about God and his wishes. Through the virtue of love and exemplary example, they followed God with heavenly voice and direction. The simple reasoning is that they listened and learnt to understand the beauty of salvation over evil and dictatorship. Intellectually, there is no easy way of explaining this.

However, God loves us all when we choose to follow the Way with virtue and love as our guide. Mankind must take responsibility for both his actions as one – *Ownership, Nirvana, and Earth* and as a connected species with life. The bottom line of this is to seek his reasoning with life thinking of others and understanding that through the seven sacraments of virtue all of his connections and reconnections with our world and the hereafter *are* affected by his actions now and in the future. To simply understand that spiritual message is our saviour with life when we truly believe in the Holy Covenants and to proactively seek to bring them into our lives. However, the distractions of greed, desire and material gain are now part of our modern century and the oversight with our Earth and her assets are now depleting the beauty of both spiritual elements and the fascination with life and fellowship.

Liberation with our faith is the tools we are all given from birth. Faith and determination are Angelic messages to us all. They can hear our requests when we seek virtue and love with our passage. Through the minefield of life, we can all know God and his messengers with the simple attribute of forgiveness and compassion for those who are in darkness of spiritual light.

Masters of Reason

The *equilateral equipoise of spiritual liberty is calculated by multiplex advancement with notable quintessence from Masters of Destiny. To reach the highest vibration and understanding is to apply divine discernment with requisite assignation, with self-awareness and correlative electromagnetic divining with God. The natural law of physics and biology will perfectly unite through Angelic interaction and sensibility of reasoning. Thus, the written word becomes united with "we" as in heaven and not personalised through individual thought processes. Through the channels of purity and light Masters can write their word through "a no thought process." This becomes true voice of spirit. Thus, the Holy Spirit can unite with pure energies of the human brain and metaphysics. The energies can then integrate with our status with truth, trust and belief.*

Elizabeth Jane Parker 2011

CHAPTER
THIRTY FIVE

DEMARCATION WITH ATTITUDE

....

"The demarcation of time is inspired, when we seek the salvation of our soul. The true connection comes with God when we adhere to Holy Spirit and the Messengers of Light. To actually compound our reasoning with virtue, we all understand the courage of our conviction and strength with belief. We find our wisdom absolves the adverse destruction culminated from opinion and disturbance to our equilibrium from our dishonourable brethren."

Elizabeth Jane Parker 2012.

....

Many *people through the modern millennia are struggling to absolve problems and defects from fellowship.* Through adverse opinion and delusion many people defy their reasoning with light. The imbalances of truth and fact are the *"Jekyll and Hyde"* disturbances that occur through good and bad evolution distorting intellectual truth and reasoning with God. Simple divine messages begin with our little acorn of hope discovering that to follow our *Masters of Destiny,* brings Angelic Forces into the arena of life and *The Way* of transcendental meaning with God. Honouring each other when we form different opinions is to know that our unification and learning teach us all about love overcoming any problems and dishonour that occur.

Through listening and knowing that God only belongs to us all through the *White Light of Reasoning* can we all truly climb the stairs of heavenly blessings!

Love and attribute are the *Lovers* of time and timescale. The journey for us all is to know that our brethren will fall into darkness and their lives become unreal with the aspect of evil luring them into dispute. Dispute is about individual opinion overseeing the divine reasoning of God. God loves all people, but he cannot intervene when individualism attempts to enforce unstructured understanding. Through uninstructed understanding from our spiritual assignation with *Holy Spirit* we will not climb the stairs of heaven. We will not find our truth with God, until our soul seeks the light of reasoning. To backtrack our footsteps will of course bring blindness of virtue when we simply disavowal *The Holy Covenants of God*.

Mankind has now reached a crisis point with God. To now find *Messengers of Light* truly means that reality and reasoning must be believed, understood and actioned. Heavenly blessings are now to be learnt again through the channels of truth and divine discernment culminating with love and lessons from heavenly source. To dishonour this is not conducive with realistic timescale and evolution.

ABSOLUTISMS
AND
HEALING TRANSITIONS

Part Three

Signs of Forgiveness

"Follow *thy way with forgiveness. For forgiveness is the gateway to heavenly blessings and God. Strive to deny the reasoning of evil intent, strive to understand the messages of righteousness. The way of God is about finding our completeness and love with all things. Healing is about our truth and resolve. Healing is about our worship of God and his virtuous way with fellowship. Healing is about us bringing love and humility into our spherical changes with evolution. Healing is about our Earth and her gifts to us all. Healing is about Angels and resolve. Healing is about our ONE.*"

Elizabeth Jane Parker 2011

CHAPTER
THIRTY SIX

INTROSPECTION WITH PROJECTION

....

*"Masters give unto your servants that which are just and equal, knowing
you have a master in heaven. Continue in prayer, and watch with the same
in thanksgiving, with all praying also for us, that God would open the door
of utterance, to speak the mystery of Christ, for which I am also in bonds:
that I may make manifest, as I ought to speak. Walk in wisdom toward them
that are without, redeeming the time. Let your speech always be with grace,
seasoned with salt, that ye may know how you answer every man."*

Colossians 4

....

Through *the intellectuality of The Universal Strategy* we all as
individuals have a responsibility towards ourselves and our
brethren within the realms of life and structure. Heavenly
vibration is ever seeking messengers of truth and reasoning for
absolving the imperfections of learning over darkness. The
darkness is every seeking people who will "host" obdurate
leanings of negativity and dishonour. We are all masters of our
own destiny seeking reform and absolve with God. To
understand our individual imperfections and contracts of
learning is simply one of challenge. This challenger is about
standing one's ground with virtuous reasoning and love. The
darkness of dishonour is now one of crisis for many.

Finding belief with God and his Holy Angels is about the creation and birth of our galvanic transition into the vibration of heavenly structure. To climb the stairs with knowledge and intellectual perspective is one of simplicity. This simplicity is about humble origins and our feet touching the earth with our love and virtue responding to the challenges for darkness. Darkness seeks the light of reasoning with kinematic energies perpetually transforming emotions into one of submission. This explanation is to provide people with *problematic weight of circumstance* that no matter how pure they may actually see themselves, within the mirror of actuality they are continually undermining their beauty and colours with repetitious malfunction when they hold to past dishonour and trauma.

The superlative qualities with our *Master's Degree* and God's teachings are to always honour our brethren. For darkness can be absolved with forgiveness and understanding dishonour. Dishonour causes blindness of virtue and divine reasoning with God and his Holy Angels. Through not accepting darkness but overriding with truth and love, we can all move away from the misconceptions and adverse effects of authoritarian opinion.

Thus, dissipating our sins with natural understanding and intelligence we can all seek Angelic assistance and resolve our abject darkness with light and love of the *Universal Strategy* and intention.

Teaching our Weakness

The *requisite adjudication for learning and life with humanity is now unbelievable with fear for many. To find a purpose through modernistic amalgamation and traumatic circumstances is the impossible task for many. Thus, to teach and proactivate reasoning will be a lesson set for many teachers of "Universal Structure" and knowledge. The message is not about fear, but to teach people in denial and scepticism about "the Universal Law of God."*

To understand our God and the messengers of virtue is to recognize that we all experience weakness and sometimes we become hard critics to ourselves and our brethren and sisters of life.

The perspective and learning within the confines of Earth and her limitations with biology, we are all set a challenge to rectify undermining thoughts about each other. As teachers of virtue, we must all culminate our understanding and knowledge with humility, honour, truth and love. Only through the sacraments of virtue can we all learn and prosper with God and Goddess of life. We must all bring a message of hope through adversity and downfall. We must all teach about truth but to understand the messages of love and divinity. This is now our journey with "Universal Structure" and foundation with life.

Elizabeth Jane Parker 2011

CHAPTER
THIRTY SEVEN

TEACHERS OF VIRTUE

....

"And Jesus he did say 'and now come I to thee, and these things I speak to the World, that they might have my joy fulfilled in themselves'."

St. John 17

....

The *forecast and prosperity of God* is about divining our souls and the completion of heavenly knowledge bestowed through great *Masters* speaking about truth, honour and love for our sisters and brethren with life. Understanding our virtues is difficult as human beings when we refuse to actually acknowledge and absolve our weaknesses. Transgressions and dishonour are often formulated through choice of reasoning the dark areas of humanity. Thus the utterance and speech of God teachings are the pellucid translations through virtue and humility. Great Teachers and wisdom is the understanding and collation of our lives when we all recognize our intellectual reasoning and collaboration of knowledge with wise and impartial translation.

The joy for us all to learn and understand is that we are all brothers and sisters alighting upon a journey with humanity, time, limitation and nature. These things give us all the knowledge through learning and understanding the words and wisdom of our *Masters of Destiny*. Our Masters in heavenly realms are no longer biological beings. They have gained their position and bearings with life by understanding the messages and lessons of life's journey. Through the purity and beauty of their heavenly lives they can teach us all to follow our star Earth and her journey around the Sun. Alignment with her essence is the humanitarian intellect performing with mortality and biological containment. Through this journey, we allow our soul to learn about the values of living with confinement and *Universal Strategy*.

We are mortal beings of creation. We are blessed through our journey when we discover our strength, courage, wisdom and compassion, love, honour and truth with our foundations. Our foundations bring us into universal status when we follow our Earth and her biological transformations and elements of time. The universal meaning for us all is to appreciate and know that we belong to God and his *Holy Messages and Messengers* with virtue. Our journey with darkness is easily dissipated when we acknowledge and understand that our weaknesses bring our divinity into a powerful transformation when we forgive and understand our brethren and sisters suffering. Through our prayers and wishes, we can overcome their darkness with love. We all know about love and virtue. The feelings and beauty of God can transform us all into philanthropic understanding and love, when we truly align our passage with Divine Message.

The love and honour of our God is available to us all to know and be. The messages to us all bring us unification and passage with light when we overcome our opinions and judgement with compassion.

Compassion is our next lesson and journey with this book. The weight of us all is about hope transforming and uplifting our spiritual passage with time. This allows us all to bring about the changes that are essential for healing our planet.

The Light of the World

Then *spake Yahshua unto them saying, I am the light of the World, he that follows me shall not walk in darkness, but shall have the light of life. The Pharisees therefore said unto him, Thou bearest a record of thyself, thy record is not true. Yahshua answered and said unto them, "Though I bear no record of myself, my record is true, for I know whence I came, and whither I go. Ye judge after the flesh, I judge no man. And yet if I judge, my judgement is true, for I am not alone for my father is with me."*

The Holy Bible

CHAPTER
THIRTY EIGHT

BIOLOGIC LAMP

....

"The light of all us begins with understanding our individualism and that associated with the "The White Light." Our heavenly Masters teach us all no matter what religion we choose. The love of God is us all when we obey the credence to love honour and obey our creed with virtue."

Elizabeth Jane Parker 2012.

....

The *way forward* for mankind is simply one of love honour and truth. This perspective with our sight teaches us all about healing our Earth and each other. We are all part of God's plan and divine discernment, however in this day and age most people *choose* to ignore divine reasoning and continue to follow a pattern which does not condone unilateral thinking as a connected element of *Universal Strategy*. Despite our adverse opinions and procrastinations with virtuous reasoning, modern man has decided that science and cynics are more believable than honourable metaphysics and evolutionary transition. The mainstay of our press and media is to relate the disasters of the worldly affairs and not abide by the good also prevalent within our world at present. The darkness of realism is much more appealing for our twenty first century. How do we as truthful beings of light understand the beauty of divine transformation with the weight of grammatical dishonour among our faiths and the love of God? The power point of absolutisms and absolve is simply about seeking our light and transformation with virtuous reasoning. This intellectual aspect of our *University of Life* is to abide by *Angels Degrees* and uphold our status quo with love.

But wisdom that is from above is first pure, then peaceable, gentle and easy to be entreated, full of mercy and good fruits, without partiality, and without hypocrisy. And the fruit of the righteousness is sown in peace of them that make peace.

James 5.

Fear must be understood by us all as *ego, this* ego will protect all other emotions that succumb to darkness. Protecting our ego is about denial and scepticism overriding the divine messages of God and his Holy Angels. Through misleading our way, the downside of sceptics brings cynicism of great bearing towards our soul. Through the darkness our soul can no longer comprehend the meanings of life's journey with divine discernment and we become lost and all energies of darkness will attempt to go against the forces of our natural reasoning and love. Does this make sense?

This is where intellectually speaking our modern age has *misunderstood* powerful reasoning of belief and God. Through adverse foundation with life and journey we as humanity become isolated from truth and reasoning with denial and doubt. This doubt causes imbalances to our virtues and we become blind with elementary learning with our set path. This is where Angelic forces seek to teach us all too simply *reset* our journey with faith and enlightenment superseding the downward spiral into one of uplifting and hope. However, again this is for the reader to decide.

Our biologic lamp follows the way with virtuous intent. Veering off course is easily assimilated with love and forgiveness. Understanding our discernment with life's ups and downs bring us all home eventually. Home is our true placement within life and connection with the Universe with trust. This trust is about overcoming severe lessons with focus and realities. This trust is to absolve all misgivings. This trust is about love, honour truth teaching our ownership within life's turmoil to overcome and succeed. However, again this reasoning is with individual choice and learning.

The love of the Universe is realism understanding our components with strength, courage, wisdom and compassion, love, honour and truth. *The Chakra Steps* ascending through life commend our journey with appreciation when we truly give blessings to all.

Wisdom, Sight and Reality

Wisdom *is the greatest simplicity of intellect. Through understanding our higher intellect we can utilize our humble origins of life's journey. Wisdom is the greatest challenger of darkness and the ignorance often perceived with the luxury of circumstance. Circumstance and comforts often bring mankind into a rheostat of rhetorical question of quiescent mind-set with the belief that God doesn't exist because "I am alright Jack!"*

There are many people suffering within our modern world today, exactly and precisely how do we understand this? The conveniences and technological advancement and luxuries now diachronic within the Twenty First Century currently excludes people who are starving and without human compassion and conscience. How do we all see this within our society of luxury but with debt and ownership precluding the love of Christ and his messages brought so long ago?

We all belong to each other. We all belong to fellowship and God. Through the avenues of disbelief we have brought divinity into one of insurrection and philanthropic dilemma with macrocosm. The question here is, if by academia and introspective interests with Earth and her science within the Universe, how do we as human beings realistically view our future? We have outlined many truths within our journey. Through our lives and incarnations with reality we have all forgotten about our one truth with life. That truth is about us living with microorganisms and biology finding our way with divine discernment and belief giving us a stronghold with God.

To see, love and honour each other overriding downside of life with forgiveness and absolve with virtue, is one big message from our creator with life. We may dislike another, but we must remember to see the good that is deep within their soul from previous incarnations and life. The darkness of karma will be overcome with self-healing and projecting our virtues with status quo. Through our troubles within our World today, we can all find God with our reasoning. We can all understand our imperfections with reality and reasoning. We can all find a way through the maze of learning and understanding about belief and faith. We can all bring about the changes needed to bring our wisdom and compassion with brethren and sisters through their own responsibility with virtuous intent,

Blessings are for all when we seek, find and maintain our love and virtues with Heaven and Earth as one element.

Elizabeth Jane Parker 2011

CHAPTER
THIRTY NINE

A GLORY REVEALED

....

*"For I reckon that the sufferings of this present time are not worthy to be
compared with the glory that will be revealed in us"*
Romans 8

....

Our *journey with life is revealed to us all every minute, hour and
second of our days.* Many questions and answers are apparent
throughout our path.

Ordinary people find imbalance and indecision with their belief.
How do we understand that to uplift this, we ask for guidance?
This guidance is open to us all with the love and compassion
from Heaven. However, once again we cover this aspect of
learning. Self-belief and inability to actually see their way
through the darkness is one of *"philanthropic dilemma!"*
Mankind has learnt to excuse individual aspirations and desires
but fails to feel compassion for sisters and brethren who have
"lost their way." Very often through modern day opinions and
media judgement is made without knowledge.

"Therefore thou art inexcusable, O man, whosoever that thou judges, for where thou judges another, thou condemns thyself, for thou that judges does the same things. But we are sure that the judgement of God is according to truth against them that commit such things. And thinks thou this, O man that judges them which do such things, and does the same, that thou shall escape the judgement of God?"
Romans 2

The uplifting of virtue is one of compassion without judgement. Through compassion our Way finds the *signpost* of love and meaning, when we learn to understand the true meaning Divine Discernment. The *Mirror of Actuality* is teaching us all about love and honour. Love and honour begins at home within our heart. Our heart beats with the rhythm of Earth and her own vibration. Through this truth we *mirror* our energies of virtue within the evolution of time and space spherically moving around the Sun.

From the above point of reference, we must all learn to acknowledge and accept the differences that many people believe but to pro activate respect and honour to all. For us to actually teach people we all work as one with the light of love and understanding. Thus, through truth and love we can all find our life with virtue through denying the discordances and distemper of malfunctioning with dishonour. All of our darkest hours can be understood when we simply understand the meaning of love and virtue with challenging downturn with love and forgiveness. This has been the greatest lesson for us all. We are all united in Heaven Realms and thus, we *do* understand the problems of the modern way.

Since the dawning of time with earth, the transformations and transfigurations with God have explored the impartiality and passive elements of existence. Through mathematical transitions of imperceptive movement, our world changes with a lanthanide series of segregated timescale and geographical movement. This movement has brought the billions of millennia into our *World* today. This *World* of beauty and gift has brought transient *eschatology* with timescale and cataclysmic eventuality. The aspect of life forms and wild life and nature itself, forming and reforming with essential scientific movement and change, we are now intellectually aware as one whole World that we all exist through the earth and her movements around the sun. We rely on upon astrophysics with timescale to understand and to perform our intelligence contained with biology. We understand that we belong to God our Father and Earth our mother through regeneration and love. We understand the rhythmic electrostatic elements of vibration and energy. We understand that we live through the gracious involvement of timescale. We all understand and appreciate our heavenly structure with earth and her life giving resources.

The small equation of each individual existing within this truth, is that we all have a responsibility to heal ourselves and that in this we can uplift each other with the benefit of God's true message to us all. We as a species need to learn about respect, honour, truth and love combining our passage with life. To understand that our responsibility is on-going and our intelligence must now be accepting the magnificence of *spiritual assignation* and the concept of science and life itself. Through the amazing transitions of science and our belief we can once more change to a better *World* of love, honour and respect for life and the reasoning of *simply being* but knowing that we are indeed a miracle of generations and procreation.

"US"
Universal Strategy

The *Heaven and Earth connection is us all following a path of wisdom, courage strength and compassion. The Tree of Life is to build our foundations with Earth structuring our growth with love, honour and truth. Within these simple words our learning becomes translucent colouration with spiritual assignation. Virtuous reasoning with Angelic affirmation and words is the simplicity of completing our journey with learning and understanding the beauty of biology and light as one being. Virtuous reasoning is the garden of beauty and vision with life and the challenges we all face. The symbolic aperture of growth is about understanding the reality and spiritual world we all aspire to. To learn about love and honour is about overriding and ignoring the delusional aspects of ego statistical elements and imagination that humanity is now impassioned with sceptical vocabulary and denial. The weaknesses of greed, malcontent, disrespect and avaricious concepts with desire are simply overthrown with respect and beauteous silence. Thus, the true wisdom with life comes without meditation when we all abide and trust the love of God within us all. God and Goddess of life is us all understanding the simple beauty of heavenly connection and devotion both to our brethren and sisters of life with love.*

The reality check with life begins with self-assertion quietly and respectively knowing our "place" with the Universal Strategy of intent and realising that others cannot see this. The realism of science and being is fundamental understanding with materialism and spiritual assignation with time. Time is the structure strategy with evolution, combining spiritual essence and feasible assets of imagination, procreating virtue and reasoning with divinity. Divinity shows us the laws of Universal Strategy and through these lessons of actuality we can pro create our understanding and belief in God our Father.

Elizabeth Jane Parker 2011

EARTH STORY
& ANGELIC PROMOTION
WITH OUR JOURNEY

....

Part Four

....

Truth and Realism

The *history of the Earth has brought us all to this point in time. Through misconception and adverse opinion we are now all waiting for a miracle. That miracle must come with responsibility and courage. That miracle must come with wisdom and respect. That miracle must come with compassion and love. That miracle is about humanity understanding and learning about our changes. That miracle is about God and Goddess of life, meaning and evolution. That miracle is about us all bringing our vibration back into alignment with God through his Holy Seraph Angels.*

Elizabeth Jane Parker 2011

The Holy Spirit of
Life and Reasoning

I saw a spirit descending from heaven like a dove, and it abode upon him. And I knew him not, but he said unto me, upon whom thou shall see the Holy Spirit descending, and remain, on him, the same which baptises the Holy Ghost."
The Holy Bible

As *human beings of intelligence* and choice we have seen the minute changes and the cataclysmic eruptions and earthquakes of history. The elemental production of geographical alignment with the Universal Structure, has presented our ancestors and forbears with a magnitude of challenge and resolve. The aspirations and intelligences of human and natural life have undergone imperceptible quantum legato structure of plate movement, within our Earth. We have also experienced the magnitude of disaster from this "unseen" action of our planetary alignment with the universe.

The human mind-set has unfortunately lost the ability to understand the forces of nature and our natural world of evolution and timescale. Thus, we all take life for granted and believe that materialistic exchange and money is the valuation of our lives during the modern era of the twenty-first century. Our current world today is experiencing both humanitarian dilemma and natural disaster around the Globe. We can experience the sensations and see this, but, however, we fail to understand that the Earth is upon her own journey around the sun. Through "Voices from Heaven" our holy alignment with

159

God was demonstrated through the power of intellect and advice, that we are all losing our path and understanding with Earth and her history. We as biology and spirit have forgotten our ancient memories and association with land, sea, air and water, of life giving attributes. Thus, our ancient messages of honour and truth through the Chakra Systems have been lost to us all as humanitarian fellowship and love with life and biology. Small energies now curtail our vibration with electrodynamism and receivers of the holy sacraments. We as intelligent beings now misunderstand the messages from God our father and Earth our mother. Yes, it is that simple but the complexity of change has brought this planet of life into crisis for human beings and all life giving forces. How do we as individuals rectify our journey with Earth and her future?

We as human beings must understand that divinity is not "airy fairy or contrary beings." The message of power comes to us all when we learn about our lives and that of Earth Mother. We are small and live within biological assets. Through the miracle of both biology and the spiritual connection with Heaven we all need to acknowledge the reality of Angelic forces and nature. We must understand that the Earth is powerful because of her life giving assets. She needs to be respected and loved through our mind-set understanding the vibrations and connections with our Chakra Systems and the responsibility we all have both to ourselves and our brethren and sisters of life.

Through healing ourselves and understanding the love of divinity is an insignia of our truth and being with God. Angelic forces are the power we seek and through them we will begin to heal ourselves and that of the vibrations of Earth and structure. We must all obey our truth and pathway through life. We must believe and understand the virtues and laws of heaven and earth through learning and understanding of God's wishes. Thus, we will eventually through the next millennia bring home to us all the love of Christ and the teachings of true religion and belief. And that belief is all creed and religion recognising that we serve one God and that God is truth, love, honour and respect. That God is about us all maintaining our belief with honour and respect for life and our brothers and sisters of diversity. That God has order through his Angels and their power. Thus, our soul will be energised through the Universal Energy Field and the intelligence of higher power.

The healing processes of our Planet and the Seraph Angels of God bring to us the power of light and karmic transference, when we simply learn to understand our own journey and that of fellowship. The criteria for us all are to once more bring peace and tranquillity into our World of One. This transition can only truly be known when we all learn to understand the processes of healing and the virtues we all aspire to when we recognise and realise the truth about life and reasoning. Wisdom is the key to our alignment with Earth and her generosity and generation of humanistic growth.

Thus our journey begins.

CHAPTER
FOURTY

ANGELIC PERPETUAL MOTION
WITH TIME

....

Angelic promotion realistically means preservation of evolution with Cosmetology and movement. Kinetic transitions and chemical formation is the actuality and reality of celestial reasoning. From simplicity to mega structure our existence still remains an eternal propensity with time. Answers and questions are formulated through an evolutionary prospectus with adjudication and natural laws of the Universe. To bring this into modernistic thought process is to relate our lives with an eternal soul of virtue. Thus, Angelic encounters through life bring us purity and universal messages. From God we all grow and understand the wonder of Angels.

Elizabeth Jane Parker 2012

....

Through *the ages of man ordinary life* has been undermined and the true message from Angels has been forgotten. To understand the messages brought by *the seeds of light* is to understand our connection and impartial engagement, with reality and reasoning our journey through life.

God is about divinity and light showing us the way forward into the future with love. That love is brought to us by Angelic Assistance and light. We can all understand the beauty and breath of God and life, when we truly embrace our reasoning with forgiveness and absolve. The foundations of our lives is to know that are truly loved within heavenly realms but only through understanding the purity of light and message can we all truly raise our vibrations into God's realms and belief. There is no short cut for humanity but with blessings and understanding we can all bring the *white light* into our lives.

Through simplicity and the inmost reaches of our soul can we bring the truth of ages back into our lives? We must question our individual aspects, as well as learning about our fellowship. We must answer God and his Angels about our mistakes and malfunctioning with the *Light of Reasoning*.

There are no wars in heaven. There is no hatred in heaven. There is no greed in heaven. There is no desire in heaven. There is no dishonour in heaven. There is no abuse in heaven. There is no disregard in heaven. Thus, only divinity through Angels and God and Goddess and *Masters of Destiny* can we truly bring the word and message of love. Through understanding the New Age we will all begin to hope and pray that the destruction caused to our Earth and her beauty can be reconciled and the resurrection truly begin.

The Wonders of Belief

Belief *and transition with Angelic Power is about self-absorption disallowing negativity to enter our spherical learning. Through our Heart Chakra we can connect with our soul and spirit as one. Thus, our soul can release energies distorting our path and confusion. We must all understand our virtues through our passage with life and learning to ignore negative reasoning but to actually see our brethren when they are in pain. For pain is blindness to our soul and the connection with heavenly voice.*

Elizabeth Jane Parker November 2011

Abide

is patience of self. We all become stressed through adverse circumstance. Abide brings forbearance into your soul. Life cannot be pressurized, we require a solution to our mind-set.

Abide means to acquire a time solution of space. The space of concept can change our truth.

Abide is the Angelic word of time. Time heals. Adjustment is change, and process is time. Abide means faith in self once more with challenge of belief.

Abide is divine understanding of the precious healing of time. When trauma enters our soul adjustment with abide is needed to realign our understanding and faith.

Prayer

O holy angels of God's blessings and peace,
Provide me with comfort during my distress
Provide for me the love of all things holy
Provide for me the holy counsel should I lose my way
Provide the joy of regeneration and growth once more
O Holy angels for I love thee
And await your love

CHAPTER
FOURTY ONE

OPTIMUM PRINCIPLES OF
UNFOLDMENT
WITH TIME AND SPACE

....

"Our journey with life is a miracle. Man has yet to even understand one small aspect of this. Through minefield of money and undermining propaganda of the modern age, we fail ourselves and that of our Earth. Through this delusional intellect we are all responsible for change and thus the equinoxes of evolution will bring to us all the truth about our historical mistakes. Thus, we begin to learn again about life, reasoning and God."

Elizabeth Jane Parker 2012

....

The *catechism of change* is about convergence with time and evolution bringing the right messages of light to us all. The realism of this is only seen through the written of God directed by *Masters of Destiny* residing in a body of light and divine truth and message. Only through abiding with acceptance of true realism and purpose can enlightenment be understood.

The responsibility and glory is about spiritual assignment with *Grand light Masters of hierarchal status* and cosmic superstructure. Humility and respect bring our assignation into divine alignment when we reach our highest vibration in life and utilize this for the knowledge and true purpose with God and his teachers. To understand the true value of this is to teach us all to know our place with virtue within heavenly construction and life's journey with time. Through angelic affirmation and articulation bring us all to recognise and realise positive elements towards our true purpose and knowledge with life's reasoning. Through understanding undermining energies, our growth with reality and reasoning our imagination can brings us to highest level of thought process and strength.

The magnitude of reasoning involves an evolution of imperceptive mathematical energies of transference. This transference is an important gratification of atoms and chemical reactions with light, water and sustenance. This then accumulates bacteria with micro-organisms into a minute spectrum of change. This spectrum brings gradual automation of energies utilizing reality and reasoning with our brain function and body of light integrating with life and timescale.

The powers of our parallel universe become a protraction of bio chemicals with unseen cosmic particles and magnetism with gravity. This attracts bio reactionary status and accumulation. The substructure and reformation with cellular growth balances invisible directives via DNA and imperceptive timescale. Our parallel universe utilizes all positive energies with our biological transformations with colour, phonetic and a bio chemical photometer organising photosynthesis with ecology and life. All connections and reactive electrodynamics conform to structured messages contained in micro substructure unfolding. Through this complicated process angels will bring gradual healing to our individualism and thus protecting all undermining ego evolutionary processes.

We all have this ability when we discover our true potential through virtuous avenues of love and light. Through our challenges we will learn to appreciate the messages from *God and his Masters of Destiny.*

Absolve

is to forgive oneself and others from the traumas of learning. Absolve brings humility and tranquillity into our soul.

Absolve is a release from turmoil and allows the mind-set of reason to accumulate once again. Absolve is a process of acceptance and change after denial has occurred. Absolve is divine forgiveness to self and others.

Absolve must evolve from an encumbrance and transgression of purpose and dilemma. Self-belief has been tested and absolve brings the soul back on to the right path of understanding.

Absolve is the opposite of denial. Denial is self-punishment. It does not aspire to truth of being, thus denial will cause trauma and confusion to our soul. Thus, one must acknowledge denial and move into the realms of absolve. Once this occurs, elevation energies can once move purity and light into the Universal Understanding element of our path. The push and pull with gravity will unite with beauty and light and the reconnection with truth. Absolve is the most powerful weight lifting element of spiritual enlightenment and understanding. Our soul can push forward into the realms of dissipating weak and unstructured energies. Thus, absolve is fundamental reasoning within the White Light.

Prayer:

Dear Holy Angels of God
Please disallow my vengeance upon my brethren
Please disallow me to blame others for their trespasses
Please bring me peace and tranquil energies
Of love, forgiveness and respect
Bless my trauma and release with purity and light

CHAPTER
FOURTY TWO

BALANCING OUR VIRTUES

....

Balancing our virtues with wisdom, strength, courage and compassion bring us to know our place of structure. Our structure brings us to know that God really exists for us all individually. His love deepens when we learn to understand our proaction against negative forces and downfall. Thus each day of our lives we can begin again and learn to understand ourselves and the world around us.

Elizabeth Jane Parker 2012

....

We *have learnt about the building blocks of life* and our existence within biology and spiritual essence. Through our purpose we can *invite the rite of passage* and alignment with angels. Through this procedure we can accustom our learning without meditation. Meditation teaches us to relieve and achieve the spirituality within and without our body but the truth of our being will not be recognized within this plane of elevation. For earthly experience will once more appear to us through our life. Elevation of *Heaven and Earth* must be obtained with realism and life's lessons of advancement. This is where we connect with the Spiritual Evolution Event. From the gift of our lives we can motivate our journey with the projection and absorption of all energies but by moving on each and every day with appreciation we as humanity can relieve the burdens of yesterday.

The vibrations and connection with Heaven and Earth are real. To trust our intuition and the teachings of God is through our existence with biology and light being as one. Thus, to move forward with light we need to exert our virtues with reasoning. This reasoning is divine within the confines of God's messages with love and virtue superseding the negative forces of darkness. Thus, through learning and understanding the words and affirmations we can move forward knowing our connections with spiritual essence and that of our foundation with earth. Through understanding angelic forces we can move through our life with love, honour and trust. This trust disallows ego and personalised interest overtaking our status quo. Somatically, we are responsible for our biology and thought process but in order to achieve the maximum benefit from universal energies, we all need to understand the reality of life and spiritual meaning. Half the story is simply not obtaining knowledge and the journey we all have with our earth and movements around the sun. Realism is about *positive thinking* and absolve. Through the benefits of positive *megawatts* and understanding the power we were all born with, is to know we cannot realistically misunderstand the *universe*.

We are today experiencing a dilemma within our world. And through this dilemma the true meaning and messages of angels are used for self-interest and *phosphorous insecurity with photochemistry and light. This causes many people to seek for them* without realising our heavenly connections through diversity and the leading light of all as one. Through disorganising strategy and individualism we lose sight and meaning of fellowship and God.

When we all realize that through each and every person upon this planet there is a purpose and life story. Unfortunately, again there many people who seek glory and personalised interest only. Angels do not understand this attraction and will not intervene unless we all bring them to us through humanitarian and the values of our planet and her assets.

Acceptance

is a truth. Acceptance is who we are. Acceptance brings great wisdom into our soul.

We all know how another can offend and offset our pride. We all know that our reaction to different realms of dishonour can challenge our peaceful mind-set. However, when the challenge is presented to us, we can all benefit from actually seeing and knowing who we truly are. We are God's children. We do as children, however, allow ourselves to deny our responsibility. In this aspect truth brings trust. Trust in our truth and to speak with respect but understand that divine truth has power. That power comes with compassion and love. Compassion can seem painful for our pride but to diminish this we must understand our *"mirror of actuality."* Compassion with truth can be painful to others; however, our acceptance and their acceptance will bring Universal Healing against the effects of dark energies seeking to resolve their commitment to doubt and dishonour to all. Acceptance and truth with compassion will bring love once more into the arena of divine discernment.

Acceptance of our individual imperfections and weakness are the attributes we require to bring the realms of forgiveness back into our lives, thus, we can move forward upon our spiritual path with purpose and love.

Acceptance is a hard lesson to learn for some. Current modern mind-sets are often too difficult to accept for many. We often believe we are right and others are wrong. This is opinion and is not conducive to Angelic Law. Angelic Law is about honour, truth, respect and love culminating through our life's experience. To acknowledge acceptance is to find love again and a better understanding of ourselves and other people. Acceptance is a wonderful lesson if ego and doubt are overcome.

CHAPTER
FOURTY THREE

BALANCING OUR VIRTUES

....

Balancing our virtues with wisdom, strength, courage and compassion bring us to know our place of structure. Our structure brings us to know that God really exists for us all individually. His love deepens when we learn to understand our proaction against negative forces and downfall. Thus each day of our lives we can begin again and learn to understand ourselves and the world around us.

Elizabeth Jane Parker 2012

....

The *light of Christ* is a journey we make in life. This life can bring to us all the beauty and sanctification of God and the universe as one whole meaning. The diversity and wonder of God's gift to us all is about our one truth and absolve with evil. Evil is not divine purpose and thus man has had the choice and foundation to absolve his dark energies with light and reasoning with wisdom.

Through our journey and time upon this beauteous and scarred planet, we now all need to unite and prosper our energies towards each other with love and honour. The heavenly vibrations with virtue are about accessing our truth and love for each other. This simple explanation has become a complex almanac of atomic weight with altercation and atmospherics against God and his Angels. The *Immaculate Conception* of learning and reasoning has now lost the symbolic terms of true love of spirit and biology as one. Understanding our individuality is about self-adjudication with virtue and the teachings of our *Holy Masters* in heaven. Thus, to bring their word mankind must acknowledge his weakness and aspire to change with virtue and love.

The love of God will never forsake us when we truly carry our virtue with love and pride. Our virtue is the treasure of all life with the *Systems Analysis* criteria of our Soul and connection with our God belongs to us all through love, truth and honouring our growth through life and reasoning. Our daily prayers and sanctification are with virtue superseding all downfalls with grace and serenity. Honouring our brethren and sisters of life is essential for our growth with virtue as our guide.

Understanding our connections is the simple acts of love and honour precipitating darkness. As before, we learn to forgive all who dishonour us. We learn to move ever forward with our Earth and her journey through space.

Acknowledge

brings acceptance of responsibility. Acknowledge is a powerful process of elevation.

Acknowledge overcomes adversity.

Acknowledge is a conclusion after a lesson of life is given by God. Acknowledge is a learning process.

Many people will deny acknowledge by ego. However, to acknowledge one's weakness is to empower self back into universal structure and learning process. Acknowledge becomes difficult when denial of truth occurs. Denial without acknowledge will bring pain to self. Denial is not truth. Denial is an opposite energy to acknowledge. Acknowledgement is empowerment of truth and acceptance of one's responsibility. Acknowledge is the Divine Understanding of reason.

To acknowledge responsibility is the lesson of belief. Belief in one's self and attributes. To deny brings shame.

The beauty of life is to acknowledge acceptance of downfall and elevate our energy into the realms of reality and reason. Acknowledge is a creative energy which empowers our soul.

Prayer:

Oh Holy Angels of love, reason and tranquillity
Bring my bearing into acknowledge and allow thine focus
Bring my heart into alignment with Earth and her energies
Oh Angels of great power and love
Bring my status into the realms of truth
Bring my understanding into acknowledge
Bless my soul and life

CHAPTER
FOURTY FOUR

HOLY SACRAMENTAL AND VIRTUE

....

We are all part of God's messages and determination. To believe and love our dishonourable brethren and sisters is the simple test of our aspirations and will with life. To overcome distortion and disbelief we follow our Star of Life, Earth. For through her gifts to us all we seek and follow her path within our Universe. She is our redeemer and future within and without Heavens blessings. Thus, through our admiration for her and her life giving attributes we allow Angelic power to bring us all home."

Elizabeth Jane Parker 2011

....

As *brother and sisters of light* we all need to balance our individual equilibrium. Through the processes of mind-set neutralising all aspects of delusion and self-deprecating imagination we can all begin again with understanding the processes of God's wishes.

Our mind-set promotion begins usually with confusion and misunderstanding our purpose. Through the avenues of influential teachings not demonstrating intelligence with *Universal Strategy,* unfortunately many people have lost their way through the *maze of life* and the reasoning of divine message. Divine message is about absolve, acknowledgement and love formulating with our individual truth. Our individual truth is not about *airy fairy exposure* with angelic message and the love they bring to us. This love is unconditional when we simply learn to recognize our responsibility and blessings with life and the *Holy Sacraments*. Strength, courage, wisdom, compassion, love, honour and truth, these are the foundations of our beginnings with divine teachings

As all spirits of life, our lessons upon Earth bring us to being our journey through time understanding the beauty of angelic words and procreating them in our mind-set of actuality. Through their pure energies with virtue we can all change our lives for better. Through individual metamorphisms within our chakra systems we can all heal our journey with time. Our vibrations will transmit this through the Earth and her vibrations and heartbeat. Through this transmission we can align our virtues with Angels and their messages. Through affirmations through our heart chakra the realism of our intentions with life, we can conjoin with divine reasoning and will. Through our determination and attribute we can appreciate our daily convergence with life.

Angels will come to us through the divine procedures only. They cannot intervene with self-interest and greed. They cannot intervene through desire, lust, manipulation and quandary of thought process and/or denial of purpose. This we must all learn and understand for the New Age. We are self-responsible for Earth and her connections to us all. We are responsible for the love and growth of our planet. We are responsible for the steps through reality and our incarnation.

Thus, healing and raising our individual vibration throughout the next millennia is the responsibility of mankind. The choice is with us all. The responsibility is with us all. The Earth is our mother we must now respect her resources. We must now respect each other.

Admire

is to see attraction. Attraction brings individuality and purpose of another. Admire is a friendship of feeling and allows us the diversity of fellowship.

Many of us admire others and their achievement. Enjoyment of another person's achievement is to share the experience of joy. Sharing experience allows self to feel admiration without envy.

Admire brings serenity of self into focus and creates a warm feeling of pleasure.

Admire is to feel divine and the pleasure of another. This energy brings unity. Admire brings comfort that we all enjoy each other as human beings.

Prayer:

Dear Holy Angels of God
Please show me the way of love without desire
Please show the assets of truth and true love
Allow my responsibility with fellowship
Allow my truth with foundation
Disallow envy and transgressions against my
Brothers and sisters of humanity
Bring me compassion and love
Bring me honour and love
Bring blessings with life
Bring me truth with all things divine
Amen

Prophesy

The New Age will dawn with great dilemma. Upon this dilemma will come 1000 Seraph Angels unto the Earth? Upon the troubled World will they bring a message and this message will bring great changes. These changes will be known to all eventually. The karmic blessings will take place among men of dishonour and honour. Through these changes will bring great earthquakes, floods and stormy seas. But through the millennia man will learn of again about Earth's powers. Man will learn to honour, man will learn to respect. Man will begin his learning through intelligence understanding the blessings from God."

CHAPTER FOURTY FIVE

THE PHYSICS AND THE PHYSICAL OF PHILANTHROPIC VIRTUE

The *physics of our planet* are ever changing through spectrum, velocity and phrenological aspect of evolution and change within and without the confines of Earth and geology.

We as human beings are but a small speck of dust within the confines of consciousness and biology. Our understanding has been a limited entrapment within the confines of *phosphorescence and philanthropic* virtues with time and space with reality. Thus our intelligences throughout the history of mankind have not exceeded the evolutionary philosophy with understanding truth. Humankind has not grown from virtue and thus his opinion supersedes the basics of humanitarian perspicuous mind-set. The wonder aspect of free thinking and learning augments opinion and dogma influencing the continuous void accumulating diametric ignorance with light.

The history of humanitarian intelligence has now become a magnitude of injudicious congestion understanding reality and reasoning the problems that our current modern world is experiencing. Mankind is ever seeking with his intelligence to blame each other for the natural changes of our planet Earth and her own biological and geological changes with evolution and time. As one objective with God we all learn to understand with our conscience and consciousness the reality of planetary connection and forces of nature. Ignorance with spiritual essence during our modern times often performs with negative and belligerent pragmatism with understanding our life's impermanence. Humanity needs to appreciate and learn about sustainability, resources and realistic aspects of life in general. The truth today is simple *we have lost sight with materialism, money and unrealistic ideas about our future realities.*

Our Earth and her journey around the sun are but a minute speck of dust within an eternal gallery of stars and our universe. The mind blowing aspect of our lives is about existing within this spectrum of magnitude and *parallel of latitude* converging with time and space. All must understand we live in a world of bio diversity and limitations.

The diversity of life is the fascination of living
Elemental transition eternally giving
Each day we awaken
A new adventure waits
Positive mind-set and learning elates

Our journey with adventure vibrates our choice
However we travel we have a voice
Downturns and upturns
Helter Skelter our way
The theatrics of living will be our play
The moment of aspiration of learning to choose
With strength and courage we cannot lose

The pendulum swings, our passage with time
With virtuous living we cannot decline
Pressures of modern living
Journey through the maze
We align our assignation through this phase
Of messages of love, consideration to know
Life is the adventure our rivers do flow
Healing with virtue our physical stress
We can assign wisdom and compassion
Giving finesse

We are at one with all things of light
We can absolve disadvantage with God's might
The Angels of mercy bring us all home
When we understand love that we are not alone
For cherish the challenge to aid and abet
God's love for us all into the net
We are but the lambs of being so wise
The symbolic meanings cannot disguise
Our love
Our honour
Our Truth

The Conscience of Conscious Memories

Our mortality is but a passing memory through our journey with this planet. Through our lives upon Earth, we all need to believe in our One GOD and his love for us all. There is no answer for people who choose not to listen. But, through our genetics and actuality with life we all need to honour and obey the natural transitions and philanthropic association with our world. We need to know that the world was here before we were born. Thus, through her history and knowledge about her journey, we all came into being.

GOD helps us all to understand this and to believe in all good things coming from destruction. For mankind will learn to love and honour our Earth and each other through recognising this. We move on with our journey but will feel the sadness that many people will feel through loss. But understand this, we are united in truth. We are united endocrines as brothers and sisters through the universe and the planets surrounding us. We must now pray for each other and understand that our journey through life will always have hope.

Elizabeth Jane Parker 2012

Aspire

means inspiration of self. Self-will aspires to mind-set of direction. This brings imagination into focus with reality. Focus aspires to create and give pro-action into thought process.

Aspire will assist our journey. We aspire to focus energy. This energy can open up our direction into the realms of understanding.

Aspire is beautiful description of our direction and journey through time. It is a creative and positive energy with timescale and solution. It brings our truth and growth.

We can all experience aspiration of thought and proactively promote this into reality. Reality becomes our trust recognized and we aspire to follow our path.

Aspire is beautiful and tranquil to our senses and perception and is divine pathway for self.

CHAPTER
FOURTY SIX

THE SALVATION WITHIN THE SEVEN
SACRAMENTS OF VIRTUE

....

*"Wherefore laying aside all malice, and all guile, and hypocrisies, and envies,
and all evil speaking, as new born babes, desire the pure milk of the word, that
ye may grow thereby, if so be have tasted the Lord is gracious.*

I Peter 3

....

The *messages of the Christ* come to us all through self-belief in all
things good and wise.

There have been many civilizations of knowledge, virtue and
worship through the mountainous millennia of creation. The
world is ever changing her geographic and zodiacal alignment
with the Cosmos. Infinity brings divinity and love with truth
we all understand our position with Earth and the here and now
of choice, wisdom and love. The simplistic aspirations of us all
are to know that we are representatives of God and his world
of spirit on the Earth. Her connections are with the entire galaxy
with whom we are reconnected.

The planetary movements and cosmic vibrations of life are
through the elements of gravity and the *master switch of
electrodynamics* with evolution and change. The imperceptive
and corrective forces of nature often bring us to blame God

when the Earth transforms through the history of timescale with affinity. The forces of nature adhere to messages from the heavens and the strategy that is composite and reactive to micro particles, the truculent activity of earth plate movement that has been changing through eternity and magnitude with spin and electrodynamics of energy.

Opinion and denial can bring many disadvantages to the uplifting of our Earth and her vibrations within our immediate cosmic connections. We all belong to reality and reasoning our seven sacraments of virtue. The meaning of life is the ever moving spectrum of change. From this simple explanation we all move with the miracle of time and space with our everyday reality. To many modern day thinkers we just exist through time with science and revelation. However there is intelligence unbeknown to us all. That intelligence belongs to our creator of all things, our God of Creation. Through his eternal love for us all our Masters of knowledge and love teach us all to unite with them and bring the light of Christ and his love for us all.

Determination

is virtue of self-aspiration with light and reasoning. Determination brings us to recognize and realize the truth of our journey and challenge. Determination is an angelic word only when we understand virtuous intentions through life.

Determination overrides all prejudice and envy with our brethren and sisters of life. And through the channels of reasoning our virtue we can all aspire with change.

Despair not when blindness occurs
Doubt not your true path
Envy not others gifts
Pride but with love and honour
Hope brings all to see
Gift comes to us all with hope and determination
Vision of truth
Vision of life
Vision of God
Vision of Goddess
Vision and God with determination and love
Wisdom with virtuous evaluation
Truth as your guide
Love as your light
Despair absolved with life renewed
Purpose with peace
God as love and light for all of humanity
God as our true meaning
God as our father

CHAPTER FOURTY SEVEN

"WHITE EAGLE" AND WE PHILANTHROPIC LOVE FOR ALL

....

"Verily, verily I say unto thee, we speak that we do know, and testify that we have seen, and ye receive not our witness. If I have told you early things, and yet believe not, how shall ye believe, if I tell you of heavenly things?"

St John 2

....

The *"Kundalini" is about us all understanding our colour and light through our Chakra Systems anointing* with the *Christ Light* conjoining with heavenly vibrations. Understanding our mind-set and *divine will* brings us all into a good place when we all rejoice and learn with heavenly vibrations and light. Through impervious transition with opinion we can all give credence with virtue. Thus, through divine intervention we can all learn that we are honourable and truthful with mind-set and bodily structure.

Through the *Holy Sacraments* the *Kundalini from symbolism* arises to the heavens forever and our body of light transfers from all evil and downfall into congruous understanding. We learn that the fruit and seed of the Earth and her soul become our condition and belief through bodily sanctification and love for each other.

And Moses lifted up the Serpent in the wilderness, even so the Sons and Daughters of Man be lifted up, that whosoever believes in him shall not perish, but have eternal life. For God so loved the World, that he gave his only begotten Son, that whosoever believed in him should not perish. For God sent not his son into the world to condemn the world, but through him the world would be saved.

The Holy Bible

How do we actually understand the symbolic reasoning of the above passage? Through this work with biblical and modern translation do we understand our ancient memory and the modernistic preferences for disbelief? We are all God's children and light, but so far along our road of history the actuality of our biological function and the treasures we all seek through challenge and resolve is not understood as humanity and one.

Reasoning our lives with wisdom combines our divine will with truth. Through this truth and *universal strategy* of intention we can every day of our lives feel good and wise, with all elements of natural life and supernatural aspirations for our reality and in the moment impervious contribution to global apathy during modernistic dilemma and opinion. Our Alma Mater, Mother Earth will bring our salvation into *universal strategy* through understanding her divine being within the Universe and Galaxies of both affinity and time.

We are all equal as divine beings of God. However, many people throughout the world today fail to find faith and enlightenment as the answers to our natural and collaborative initiation into the realms of life with interest and fascination for all things of creation. We all take for granted the almanac of *the here and now* affecting our future. We all misunderstand that by simply forgiving and letting go of all negative elements of personality and individualism, we can move forward and uplift the natural vibrations of our conscious and conscience with life. This is yet a mystery for mankind to believe in but through the next millennia and the Earth's movements with time and connection with our galaxy, we will all teach our children the rights and wrongs of dilemma. Through understanding our responsibility and co-existence with God, we will eventually understand the beauty and light of our Earth and the Universe.

We are all part of this plan but as yet we fail to bring light and understanding to the heaven and earth connection. We must all deny the reasoning of ego and the weight of circumstance we all currently carry through the twenty first century. Through finding our intelligence as one, we will all rejoice again in the future with the shift of negative elements throughout the globe.

Our mortality is but a passing memory through our journey with this Planet. Through our lives upon Earth, we all need to believe in one GOD and his eternal love for us all. There is no answer for people who choose not listen. But, through our genetics and actuality with life we as humanity need to honour and obey the natural transitions and philanthropic association with our world. We need to acknowledge that this Earth was here before our birth. Thus, it is through her history and knowledge within time and space we all came into being.

God helps us all to understand her journey with ours and believe that all good things are reborn again. For mankind must now learn to love this Earth and her gifts to us all. We are united endocrines as brothers and sisters through the Universe and the planets surrounding us. We must pray for each other and learn that our journey will always have hope through the dilemmas of life and reasoning.

Effulgent

is one meaning of balance and radiance. This angelic meaning is about balancing our energies with colour and light. Thus, through God and the teachings of virtue we can connect every day with our Seraph Angels of light and reasoning, through learning and understanding the lessons of life and the journey we all undertake. Through our Chakras and Angelic intervention we can all find our status and position with Heaven and Earth. The sword of truth will bring us all a resurrection with Christ.

Behold, happy is the man and woman that GOD corrects,
Therefore despise not thou the chastening of the Almighty
For he makes sore, and binds up:
He wounds and his hands make whole
He shall deliver thee in six troubles:
Yea and upon the seventh sacrament no evil will touch thee.

Thus, effulgent brings us all to understand the importance of our Chakras and alignments with atoms and the orchestration of life and energy.
Effulgent is about balancing our life force with the Earth and her energies with time.

Oh Holy Angels of Christ
Allow me to enjoy my life with balance
Allow me to understand the breath and beauty of wisdom
Allow me to understand my courage
Allow me to find my strength
Allow me to give compassion in times of trouble

Allow me to be honourable
Allow me to be a truth
Allow me the true love of God

Our Father

CHAPTER
FOURTY EIGHT

TRUE LOVE AND REASONING

We *are all on a journey with God* and the lessons apparent to us all, honour and respect within the partitive measures of the written word instruct us all to know and understand that truth is necessary for the healing progress.

Our messages from Heaven are about healing our modern mind-set and attributes for life. To teach about humility, honour, truth, love and respect is to know that our *Mirror of Actuality* represents our humble bearing to the World. We learn to know that *God our Father* brings our lessons into absolve through *understanding* the challenges beset us all. These challenges are against the effects of ego need to be *recognized and realised* to our bearing and consonance within the aspects of biological containment with virtue.

Healing all darkness's of life is one of simplicity. However, to understand simplicity and love has been the blindness of all people seeking to release their burdens through life with denial and disbelief. Healing our Planet has become an *Electron Microscope* dissipating elementary particles and becoming caustic vibration with denial and disbelief. Denial has precipitated global *apathy*, about our association with *delusionary anthropocentric ideology*. Even through the *Christian Faith* arguments occur and the forum of choice becomes divided through misrepresentation. Through self-opinion with *antinomian idealism* has become one of dishonour as part of creed and opinion! Thus, the unfortunate *ploughing of seeds and scatter* of the harvest festival obtaining the wonder and beauty of growth becomes a complicated transition and unbelievable discrimination for *Holy Message* of God.

We as holy communicators to the World must understand that God is part of us all and through example of humility, love and self-belief in his virtues, we can truly work with Heaven and Earth. Understanding our journey through time and space is *about* mind, body and spirit as an organised and proactive element.

Again, meditation is a *"school of thought"* regarding spiritual assignation and levitation of mind-set. However, the *Spiritual Evolution Event* is about reasoning our realities and passage through life. The beauty that exists upon our planet is slowly diminishing with the darkness of ever increasing materialism and denial. The technological advancement through our world of humanity is slowing dissipating the fascination of learning and intelligence with life. Metaphorically speaking virtual reality has taken the world by storm!

The true gift of sight is about appreciating all aspects of growth and bio diversity. Our planet of beauty over the multi millennia spectrum has brought to us resources. However, realistically these resources in a modern age cause imbalance to our environment. And despite our medium output imploring us to review our thoughts about our future, we fail as humanity to harmonize virtue in sustaining our balance between nature and desire.

These lessons are yet to be heard by humanity as a reality within time structure. Time structure has been the metamorphic effect through space. This took time, imperceptive time with micro dynamism and electrons. Reality takes time. All elemental strategies take time. Thus, at present the alarm bells of time are ringing for us all! There is no quick fix with scientific fact and from this truth we must now all re-learn our intelligence with life. We must all now seek the treasures of learning with virtuous intelligence and reasoning. We must now all SEE the Earth with God.

Elizabeth Jane Parker 2012

Providential

is divine work for understanding and proactively engaging positivity and volumetric teachings from God. Through our *Masters of Destiny* we work with spirit only. Through this connection the true voice of reasoning brings purity of light and the word of God.

Providential teaching is about us all learning and understanding our *Chakras* and the elevation and stairway to heavenly blessings. Through releasing our darkness back into light we all learn about the wonder and interest of life and reasoning.

To reach the highest vibration is simply only allowed through the learning eye of reality and wisdom superseding with providential focus and direction.

Thus, this word brings us the knowledge and allowance to work with our heavenly source every day of our lives.

Thus, providential is not inspired through meditational procedures and the light of reasoning is only truly acknowledged with reality and reasoning through our biology and light combining spiritual essence with intelligence and "in the moment" acceptance of our journey. Thus, Seraph Angels can only "repair" our Chakra systems with colour and light understanding the realism of learning and the proaction of bodily determination with karmic negotiation through challenge. Thus, hierarchal teachings then accumulate and accentuate our purpose with Heaven and Earth. Thus, we understand how the "big see" actuates and procreates our spiritual path with enlightenment.

Synchronic Theory and Synonymous Revelation With Earth

Elizabeth Jane Parker 2011

The *"Synonymous" reasoning of human translation with Divine word is about us all, the word of salvation understands the beauty of writing without peremptory resonant post graduate history. Angelic affirmations and the creative "white horses" of absolutisms surrounding our light with God are simply by extrasensory perception and hearing with virtue. The waves of hydrosphere bring us to realise our fragility with life and learning. Great powers are at present in force. Our Earth is changing her geographies.*

Through the magnetic attraction surrounding the Earth's core her plate movement extends to us all eventually. Through this concept mankind will realise that Earth moves on her journey no matter what, how or why we perceive her power! Money, greed, abuse and dishonour have no influence upon her bearing and structure with time. Our values as humankind will eventually learn and appreciate that these changes bring natural evolution and the imperceptive assimilations through universal strategy and creation. We have lived through many traumas and changes with our planet. We as humanity are all part of her progression and journey. Through our journey with her we have overlooked her beauty and gifts to us. Our intelligence has now within the 21st Century forgotten this as spiritual beings related and born through biology. Through the scientific splendour of God, our Universe has been overlooked with denial, greed and malcontent for materialism.

The attractive elements of appreciation have been dissimulated by man's intelligence. Greed is the foremost transitional aspiration of the modern world. Transcendentalism with spiritual advisors has been considered a "taboo" subject with scientists and contribution of knowledge accumulated. However, the truth is that Masters of Destiny work with Seraph and Arch Angels understanding and enforcing the Laws and Attractions of Earth and her life giving components. The hidden veil between life and spirit is mysterious to many. The failure to understand that life is fragile and we are but a small perishable aspect of the great galaxies of time and space. Our intelligence as mankind is but an impermanent perspective through ignorance and denial and the true meaning of knowledge becomes lost. God assumes many facets of delivery, and through his eternal love for our planet we must all understand our fellowship, nature and geographical spectrum with eternity. God does exist through each planet of the Universe. Our Universe, our Galaxy and our home called

Earth! We are all living a miracle of time and space identifying with each particle of existence grown both from creation and the time aspect of eternity. The dishonour upon our planet has not grown through the spiritual beauty and message of truth and religion, politics and philosophy.

Through the millennia we have existed as mankind; we as one have not learnt and loved each other. We have not understood the creative and imaginative aspects of our mind with metaphysics. Our Earth is changing, we must all begin to learn and believe again in our virtues with life and reasoning.

CHAPTER FORTY NINE

INFINITY, VOLUMETRIC AND BEGINNINGS OUR HOME, EARTH

....

"There is gold and a multitude of rubies, but the lips of knowledge are a precious jewel"

St John 2

....

How *do we all see a beginning?* Our planet has grown from infinity through light, darkness and universal strategy with time and infinite orchestration. The beauty of the Universe has brought this moment in time for us all. Exactly what indeed do we understand about our creation and the beginnings of life upon Earth?

Many theories and instruction are given us through universities, study and revelation. However, through the windows of time itself, things have changed beyond comprehension of mankind and his intelligence upon Earth. Our hazy reconstruction has formulated many theories and scientific phenomena through instruments of great power seeking and seeing vast expanses of space itself and the planets contained within galaxies beyond and near. The question is, how many planets can Scientists perceive from telescopic vision that contains water? How many planets have landmass with life? How many planets have a history that we know of? How many planets have creation and evolution with life? What do we do know about the Earth and her history since her birth? What do we know about formation and the early signs of life forming with creation? What do we know about the first signs of mankind and his supernatural intelligence upon Earth? What do we have as evidence of early beginnings with our Planet? *From a ball of fire* she evolved with violence and molten rock. From this period and her cooling down into reason, what do we understand and actually have with proof and facts substantiating with evidence of time immortal?

The fascination of history and research remain the mystery. This is where we learn to understand from the ancient history and the now of life. In symbolic terms, we know of our beginnings within heavenly spheres but from learning from history we find reasoning and light with virtue. The true light of the universe is actually impossible to research. However, there are findings and revelations about distant planets. From our Earth and her beginnings we as human beings are a minute aspect of time and reality. Our brain brings us messages of intelligence but to understand, we all actually need to believe in our being and structure with *now*. Learning from the past and conjoining our spirit and soul allow us all to configure our reasoning with life and our future sustaining light with the Earth and her resources. We all seek our treasures within life, but to actually understand our impermanent life within biology becomes difficult for many to perceive. Our lives are eternal within heaven and earth and our belief must begin again with virtue, lessons and the foundation of life and biology.

Many misunderstand their virtue and life. This sadness brings them into a place that does not inspire and fascinate them and others through the wonderful spectrum of reality and reasoning. The sadness of many people believing that they know the answers to the questions of our mortality, is not kindling the fire for knowledge. For the true thirst in metaphor, is to know that our intelligence is ever seeking questions and answers about the mystery of our planet together with her past transformations with time. Revelations of history bring many tutors to teach us through their eyes and ears with intelligence and knowledge from heaven. However, we as individuals all have our own ideas with this, and through understanding our place within *Universal Strategy* we can all wonder at our gift with knowledge and truth showing us the way forward into the next millennia.

We continually seek answers and reasoning thus, through our journey with life we can learn and pro create our knowledge without opinion. For wonder and fascination bring our knowledge to appreciate the beginnings of a new era. Our *new era is about to begin and through messages from all universal* powers we will find our Earth and home to be resourceful, fascinating and loving to our needs and ventures.

November Days
Woodstock
Oxfordshire, England

Elizabeth Jane Parker 2011

Sunny days brings our thoughts to distinguish
The village of Woodstock, quintessentially English
Today the air is cold and damp, but the sun shines through
The day begins our adventure too!
To walk from "The Bear" along the street
"Good Morning" we say to those we meet
The imposing gates of Blenheim Palace, so grand!
An opulent impression to our vision they stand
Through the archway we can espy
The picturesque scenery to our eye
No amount of visits to this place
Can ever remove the marvellous grace
Of Bleinheim charm with elegant reception
Where ever one walks with marvellous perception

The geese upon the grass reside
The Heron in flight he seeks to hide
From the lake the swans alight
Difficulty in obtaining an overall height
Flying with wings with perpetual motion,
Loud and whirring with noisy commotion
Elegant beauty flies with aviation of size

With inherent skill they can arise!
With laws of average against their weight
Flying with speed they negotiate
The marvel of legated span
The fascination of this is, simply they can!

The lake reflects with glassy projection
The mirror image of reflection
Tranquillity and peace to sooth our soul
Gently through the grounds we stroll
The trees has shades of browns, yellows and russet leaves
The deciduous plants gradually relieves
With seasons change and disappearance
The scene becomes one of adherence

The magic of this place brings our minds
Projecting impressions and absorbing our finds
"Blenheim" the building of grandeur bestows our view
The glorious statement we can imbue
The colours around the buildings observance
Different sights and resurgence
The imagination and meaning of this day
Is a wonderful experience in every way?

The Statues portray nudity and exposure
However, the "Italian Garden" gives them composure
To the "Secret Garden" we walk
Discussing previous visits, we excitedly talk
Nature's summer is depleted this year
But in spring will again reappear
We see the Pheasants in number parade

From our walk to the magnificent cascade
Beyond the sight of water doth swell
Emitting the muddy watery smell

We walk along the narrow road
Bypass the lake we have often strode
Many birds sit in flocks upon the lake
Seagulls, Grebes, Moorhens, Ducks to take
The calling of nature's natural abode
The waters of time cannot erode
Compliance with beauty upon this scene
Calm, tranquil and peaceful serene

From every angle our sight is involved
With enrichment and treasures to be resolved
With experience and pleasure of proactively seeking
The marvel of beauty and nature for keeping
Upholding these treasures both within and without
Our messages of life should always be devout
With seeing, hearing knowing our world
So preservation and enjoyment unfurled
Each and every wonder we see
We know tomorrow can always be
Stored for with our soul with preservation
And intention with God's creation

Our journey is always beginning with time
From each experience we can all always define
Whatever we feel with justification and love
We walk with God hand in glove
For many great people have contributed with pride

The foundation of virtue with God by their side
To remember the good and the beautiful assets of living
We can also contribute towards the giving

God is everywhere with faith and with essence
Upon the Earth and Heaven renaissance
He gives to us all with comfort and love
For our Mother the Earth and her great beauty
Eternal magnification
Eternal sight
Eternal Belief
Eternal Truth

CHAPTER FIFTY

THE LONGEVITY OF PEACE CALM AND HEALTH

....

"Let food be thy medicine and medicine be thy food."

St John 2

....

Understanding *the universe* is to look with projection with compassion, but to appreciate our mind, body and spirit as one element contained within a magnitude of time and space. Our bodies bring many complications to our path. Thus, to find true love with all aspects of mind, body and spirit often brings great challenge to our belief and love itself.

Love is about truth. Love is about us. Love is about growth. Love is about trust. Love is about God. From this statement many sceptics will find opinion and argument. Science and study must be about fact overriding the unknown elements of existence. Searching and studying must conclude with evidence. Evidence is about belief and knowledge. Thus, how can we see love? How can we know belief? How can we grow with this knowledge every day of lives? However, how do we as individuals explain to our brothers and sisters who deny and maintain scepticism find their life of love and intention understanding their status within God's plans?

Despite the miracle of everyday living many people have

little knowledge about how our body works. We own our individual biology but we fail to understand the maintenance aspect of how we actually work. The benefits of the medical profession are available for us all, however, how have we been shown in a modern society of intelligence to actually appreciate and understand the workings of our body and the wonderful aspect of the mechanical motivation through sustenance and maintenance? Where do we actually understand from our small beginnings as a child through to adult years the changes we will make through growth, love and sustainability? How do we appreciate the humble beginnings of our seed through the aging process to our finite lifespan?

We all contain atoms associated with the miracle of life itself and the growth of our body through universal union and love. However, the disorganized aspect of this diversity brings many avenues and roads of life to encounter. Thus, from our humble beginnings our incarnation through life must negotiate ohms of challenges to our very creation and being, we are fragile and occupants of biology. This in itself is a marvel but contradiction to our welfare and growth. The science of our perishable matter is about volition and ownership collaborating with responsibility. How are we taught from minor to major about this? How are we by modern day standards appreciative of our life and reasoning? The vortices of modern translation and life is augmented by our intelligences and learning from our humble beginnings. Thus, through our lives can we appreciate and learn from history, our parents, teachers and society about responsibility for our well-being and that of our future?

It must be accepted that we will eventually grow older. But through this do we grow wiser? Through learning and sustaining our status quo with life will allow us to bring our belief and knowledge through life for the betterment of our health through milestones and the very food we eat. Our cells within our body are a miracle of unseen phenomena and growth. To maintain and secure our lives we must understand that these miracles need to be loved and secured. Health and mind-set are very much an *orchestration of light* and life through healthy sustenance and maintenance. Can we all learn to humble our lives with the knowledge that our food is brought by Earth and her elements. The superstructure of water and hydrous containment allow us all to realise the wonder of this as a *life force* and transition with a living miracle with time. Yes, us all.

How do we in modern times understand that we are all gifted through our surroundings and availability of food and water? How exactly do we understand this small fact of everyday living? Can we bring our humble intelligence to know that our lives are a natural force of energy and sustainability? This lesson is for us all to recognise and realise as spirit and connection throughout our world of one we are humbled by the very life we live with Earth. Thus, we begin in understanding our light with God and Goddess of being. Our supernatural intelligences and heartfelt reasoning must begin with this fact before truth.

Our connection with the Earth is about reality and reasoning through the challenges we all face with life. However, do we really see this? Can we appreciate the ups and downs with reality teaching us all about belief, status and love? To carry our burdens bring many to weigh down the Earth and her truth. Through the jungle of reality we all have to carve our way and release the negative aspects of learning. God is about us all overcoming our inability to actually see our light with life and reasoning. Thus, we move into a spherical irreproachable format with change and absolve. Our current modern World needs this lesson now. We exist as matter through Earth and her gifts to us all. This is fact and truth.

Oh

Holy Angels of God
The Heaven and Earth Connection
Of light and reasoning and the love of God
Bring me love and light through truth & God
Bring me hope and virtue of all lessons from God
Bring me your blessings with honour truth and love
Bring me beauty light and wonder through all avenues
Bring remedial and blessings through the virtuous love of God
May my life regain the steps of heavenly love and embrace the light?
May the tree of life extend branches with nature, respect and honour?

V

CHAPTER FIFTY ONE

COEVAL UNDERSTANDING WITH COMPOUNDS

....

*"The soul is the same in all living creatures although the body
of each is different"*

St John 2

....

The *chromosomes concerning our very existence* are synchronized by congenital decoding through mathematical advancement with isotropic compounds with growth.   How do we understand this as a miracle? The initial thoughts and reasoning behind spirituality is to know our connection through biology and the (D2) symbol regarding the mass equals of isotropic physics of reality. The hydro containment of life is the simple compound of fluidity and solidity combining electrodynamics with atomic mass formed into a complicated potential difference of formation and shape. From this explanation how do we as human beings understand how this has evolved through time, space and reality? We then ask how did *Hippocrates* know about the genetics of our body but quotes the reasoning of the soul?

He lived in a time that we know about. Physicians of today, use the *"Hippocratic Oath"* as their insignia and meaning of healing. His knowledge was understood and began with his teaching other physicians. How do we learn about a man who lived centuries behind us? Our modern world has grown with the knowledge and the healing of the human body. We understand about medicine and surgery. We understand the makeup and biology of our human structure. However, how do we as human beings connect with a spiritual world we cannot envisage without fact or proof?

The light of our being is indeed one of connection through our bodily mass. The miracle of this brings us tools. We are born with many assets to our advantage with life. Through our mind-set we can utilize our body of movement and change. We can learn and grow with the time allotted to us all. We can learn and appreciate the miracle of our growth and demise with time. There are no endings or beginnings through space and life upon our Earth. However, unfortunately despite the miracle of life during the *twenty-first century* we still misunderstand how and why we use biology, growth and reasoning within our internal universe and the outer physique of this marvellous planet of life and beauty. We as human beings often fail to appreciate with our natural intelligence and the beauty that is both around us and our individual matter with life. Our bodily structure and mass is indeed an isomorphic collaboration with time and space every micro second of life. Our soul is born again through the science and spiritual element of cosmic learning and rotation of our Earth and her journey through the Cosmos. From this, what do we all exactly appreciate from our own journey and our life with God?

Visualize the colours and the fish in the oceans of time. Visualize mountains, lakes and sunset and sunrise. Visualize the beauty of our planet in her most wonderful glory. Imagine and visualize the ocean that has grown through eternity providing sustenance and life upon this Planet. Imagine the crystal blue waters of the tropics and the sea life of corals, turtles, dolphins and whales. Visualize the ocean with rippling waves upon the white shores. Visualize the ocean and her association with the stars above, bringing her elements to change and provide water and fluid for hydrous containment with life. Our Earth and her diversity is the ever spinning truth of our being with life. Our spirit is pure within heaven but to understand the journey of life, the encounters and challenges we experience both in understanding our self and the universe is to know that God exists within us all.

Our soul has no beginning and no ending. Our soul is the seeker of knowledge and being. Our soul is beauty, colour and light. Our soul is about truth, wonder and existence. Our soul connects with all things. Our soul is about love. Love of eternal knowledge and growth. Our soul is about our Earth and her journey. Our soul is truth. Thus, all angelic forces can exist with us and for us when we understand our journey with love, truth, honour, humility and balance. Through this concept we can utilise our lives with belief. Belief in all things that is good. Yes, despite the dishonour, ups and downs we can regenerate our soul every day with this thought, we are all loved and cherished when we truly understand virtue with all things.

"Just as treasures are uncovered from the Earth so virtue appears from good deeds, and wisdom appears from a pure and peaceful mind. To walk safely through the maze of human life, one needs light of wisdom and the guidance of virtue."

Buddha

"Nothing can cure the soul but senses, just as nothing can cure the senses but the soul."

Oscar Wilde 1854-1900

CHAPTER FIFTY TWO

THE TETRAHEDRON AND ELECTRODYNAMICS AND GALVANIZATION

....

"There is one body, and one Spirit, even as ye are called in one hope of your calling, one Lord, one faith, one baptism, one God and Father of all, who is above all. But unto every one of us, is given grace according to the measure of The Christ."

The Holy Bible

....

The *science of our light* and road with life is brought to us all through birth, transition and through natural dexterity with virtue. However, the challenges beset us all from the beginning or our lives, is indeed a challenge with biology, sustenance, and genetics through processes with learning. We are born into a world of knowledge that has been concurrently compounded with previous history and past philosophical analysis. There are many theories and research to be taught. There is always eternal knowledge to be learnt. It is not ordained that we know everything. Through the passing of time with biology our lives have transformed from implausible influence or research analytically proven to be fact. Spiritually and intellectually our world at present is confused to what exactly belief involves at a realistic level of interpretation and exactly what is the criteria for our world changing.

We all have a body of light through which we all can associate and learn from with virtue. However, modern day society brings many diversions and theories to the truth and knowledge regarding heavenly blessings. For to know that we are fellowship and united with our biology and current existence, so many people have a wonderful gift with life and reasoning and utilize their wisdom to bring growth and change unto our Earth and her own spirit conjoining with our soul. In this, we must all appreciate the spiritual voices from heaven. Teaching us all with honourable power and virtue bringing us all to know that there is a life beyond our current existence.

The *major domino* of our being belongs to our Masters residing in heavenly domains. Thus, the credence of reality and knowledge can only remain within the realms of eternity. Eternity holds both the teachings and contracts ordained from birth, thus many people cause much trauma within their lives when they refuse to acknowledge divine discernment is channelled through a portal of dimension, only through virtuous truth and honour to all men and women. So many people who actually believe in spiritual transformation overlook the knowledge and information that is given through divine discernment. They come to believe that they hold the knowledge of eternity and that they alone are the glory God! Through coming to know *Jesus of the Christ* many confuse themselves that they are actually his divine being on Earth. This is misunderstanding of true purpose. However, through this misconception they simply deny the channel and association of Heaven and the connection we all have from birth grounding our foundation with virtue. *The Glory of God* is us all following a path of blessings without desire and greed or abuse. Through imbalance many spiritual seekers have received spiritual voice and ignored the messages received. The symbolic terms of this bring them ego. Thus, the law of nature and attraction draws them away from their door of actuality, focus and devotion to God and his Angels. They mislead their passage into darkness which will take them on a journey without light. This is the sadness of ego.

For us all to channel the prosperous and beautiful light of God and Goddess of light has brought many people to sacrifice their lives. This sadness is not about martyrdom and hate, this sacrifice as shown by *Jesus our Lord* in heaven that he understood the light of our universe, God and Goddess of truth and being. This taught us all to understand that we all truly belong together as one mighty fellowship with love, honour and truth. We all belong to Heaven and Earth through the powers of divine discernment overriding the malfunction of ego and downfall.

Our *Chakras* are the unseen science of light. Thus, our soul can unite with Earth and Heaven through divine discernment and the passable aspects of virtuous karma. The ever increasing spectrum of our health, mind and galvanization is the challenge we all face with life. We all need to recognize and realize our responsibility to ourselves as one individual but to know our foundation upon the Earth and hear reasoning from our biological mortality. Our Masters guide us together with all Angelic forces when we obey and learn from the messages both within and without our journey with time. Thus, the *Christlight* is the eternal message of Heaven and Earth. We reign supreme through the virtuous channels of strength, courage, wisdom and compassion, love, honour and truth

"All I can do, you can do"

Jesus Christ

CHAPTER
FIFTY THREE

OUR GOD OF LIGHT, OUR GOD OF
REALITY OUR GOD OF LOVE

....

*"Beloved, let us love one another, for love is of God, and every one that loves
is born of God and knows God."*

I John 5

....

The *Human Light* of reality is about us knowing and achieving
our revelations through the experiences of life and reasoning.
However, many fall by the *"wayside"* of misconception and
influence. Many people mistake enlightenment and knowledge
as an isolation process and believe that they are the chosen few.

*"If we love one another, God dwells within us, his love is perfected in
us. Hereby, know that we will dwell in him and him in us, because he
has given us our spirit.*

I John 5

From this section of the *Holy Bible* how do we create this in our
daily lives? There is so much dishonour and ill among our
fellowship during the *Twenty-First Century*. Despite the coming
of our *Lord Jesus* two thousand years ago, how did we as

Christian belief utilize and procreate his message? How do we stand united today with love and honour among men? Jesus gave his life to show us all the fragility of human concept but in doing so, proved that God is indeed alive in us all when we understand his purpose and message through *Holy Angels and Jesus of the Christ himself.*

God is indeed among us all if we so choose. We are all gifts from *Heaven and Earth.* Belief in our good and that of others is about seeing and believing that we exist through God and Goddess of Holy Communion. *Love thy neighbour* is a difficult phase to encompass when we feel that we have been dishonoured. However, to overcome this we must understand that each person with whom we encounter who is caught in the net of impolite message is in fact a testament to our divinity overcoming the disgrace of dishonourable intentions. Through this aspect Jesus suffered through dishonour to his innocence and message of God's light. Through dishonour and disbelief regarding his beauty and truth malicious intent ridiculed his person with cruel example.

We are all part of the Earth, elements, universe and creation. From the symbolic reasoning of this passage we begin to understand that mankind and his association with God transcends into the glory of divine message when we simply listen. Our inner sanctum with the Earth was indeed a miracle of time and space. However, our responsibility regarding the Earth and the sea is indeed one of saving grace and virtue for the meaning of Angelic messages to us all. For we do indeed belong to a greater spectrum of reality and through this reality we must all understand our challenges, absolves and reasoning with life and balances of our quadrilateral manifestations with Earth and Heaven.

Fear is not conducive to reasoning. Through wisdom and compassion we may further our passage with light through converging our light with each other and respecting the challenges of ill intent and the conversion of forgiveness and love for any miscarriages of justice we feel from our brethren and sisters of light. We are all blessed with Angelic energies and light upon our divinity understanding and procreating our virtues with life.

For our future and love upon this planet of life we all need to teach our children to respect honour and obey the causes and effects of understanding how our Mother works. For our very future and life upon this planet is to reverse the damaged caused by us all? For we must all take responsibility and learn again to give and receive with balance.

"They claim this mother of ours The Earth, for their own use, and fence their neighbours away from her, and deface her with buildings and refuse."

Sitting Bull – Native American

CHAPTER FIFTY FOUR

QUANTUM MECHANICS – TRUSTING THE UNIVERSE

....

"Verily I say unto thee, all changes are beholden to trust. This trust is about believing in good. This trust is about our truth formulating and creating a structured foundation with virtue."

....

We *are a light. We are a truth. We are of God.* Thus, to deny our beauty and being the human race has been forgotten. From this dishonour to our spiritual enlightenment we as philanthropic understanding must remain humble and true. The centuries and millennia carry our love as one being. The spiritual assignation with light is about understanding and forgiving those that lose their way.

The truth of life will eventually catch us up if we as beings of light forget our origination with God. Our life is about learning and seeking the messages of divine knowledge. Seraph Angels of magnitude oversee the structure and foundation regarding our Genesis with light and reality.

Jesus of the Christ compelled humanity to know that *"the door is always open."* However, intellectually this does not discriminate through choice. We learn that the sadness is loss about us all. The sadness that through individual eyes, ears and senses they deny the reality of light and God himself. Christian belief has gone through many misunderstandings about what is right. However, wars, hate and denial bring our twenty-first century to know that we are divided in both understanding and belief. The messages to us all are about our beauty through learning and accepting the challenges that we must endure. The endurance test of light is absolution and divine reasoning.

The sadness of our world is about criticism, procrastination and belief in individualism as being the glory of God. In this, Jesus Christ gave his life to show the world that through his suffering we would realise that he as martyr was indeed human philanthropy and light. His messages were not about being a God but about being light within humanity and reasoning. This Easter presents itself as hope for our future. Today is the 19th April 2011 and our world is divided. As the saying goes "*United we stand, divided we fall.*" Thus, this is not about fear or retribution this is about taking responsibility.

Responsibility is about our association with humanity but to take ownership for our individual aspirations. Our Lord of the heavens chose to bring us all to know that through his light, we can understand his message. His message is about us all respecting, loving and knowing our associations with God and humanity as one. Thus, through him we as Christian believers can understand the mistakes of history.

Humanity has a role of responsibility that has now become critical for the very survival of spiritual love and hope. During 2011 humanity is currently living with denial. That denial appertains to monetary power and control. How do we all take responsibility with so much greed apparent today? How do we begin to understand the messages of *Jesus Christ our Lord in heaven*? How have we understood the unity of all men and women of holy worship through the avenues of virtue? How do we begin again as one whole body of light across the globe? How do we all live and learn with so much disservice to God and his messages to us all? How do we understand and formulate our love and hope with a world lost to darkness? These questions will be answered. Yes answered, when we begin to listen to responsibility and reason. We can all begin every day of our lives when we all learn to forgive and love our world once more with virtuous intention and belief in all things good.

"It is a great consideration for me to remember that the Lord, to whom I had drawn near in humble and childlike faith, has suffered and died for me and that he will look upon me with love and compassion."

Wolfgang Amadeus Mozart

The Power of Love

"**The** *power of love and reasoning belongs to us all when we simply listen to virtue. For virtue is the "stand post" and stability of spiritual transformation into the realms of truth and knowledge. To know our truth is real and honest belongs to individuality. The truth of dishonour belongs to ego. Love only reigns true with absolve of weakness and through Angelic Dissipation we can aspire to hope. Hope is the flower of change and thus the seeds of light scatter through our planet. These messages are important for us all to know and learn. This must be recognised and realised before release and burden can be blessed and recycled by Seraph Angels."*

As Jesus of the Christ spake, "Whatever you ask in prayer you will receive if you have faith. Blessed are those who have not seen and yet believe."

Elizabeth Jane Parker 2011

THE SPINTRONICS OF ACTUALITY & INTENT WITHIN THE SPECTRUM OF CHANGE

....

Part Five

....

CHAPTER
FIFTY FIVE

UNDERSTANDING ALL
ASPECTS OF VIRTUE

....

"In him was life, and the light was the life of men. And the light shines in the darkness, and the darkness comprehended it not."

The Gospel according St. John

....

We *are all of God's children* and to understand this praise from the *Holy Bible* is to comprehend that we all have responsibility for our individual light and that of all. *Angels of All* represent one whole body and the life aspect of learning. The Angel within us all can only truly be obtained through our passage with life and learning about virtuous intentions. Every day of our lives within biological containment we live a miracle with time. From this we can appreciate our immortality with life and learning, absolving all undermining messages and mistakes from our brethren and sisters of life.

We are now beginning a *New Age* of change. This change is about us as humanity learning to live with our Planet of beautiful gift and life. The darkness of humanity is prevalent at this time of celebration for Easter 2011. To record this statement is know that we have a future but mankind will need to change. This change is about responsibility, learning and observing the mistakes we are all prone to make. From mistakes throughout the next millennia we can make a change. We can learn from *Jesus Christ* and his sacrifice of life. He gave the ultimate price of his belief and teachings. His declaration "*that he was the light of the world*" was to give us all a message that as ordinary people he will show us how and why. As an ordinary human being his message to us all was about love, light and reason. His greatness was about his love of humanity and the suffering many people incurred during their life. Through the forgotten channels of mortality divinity was lost to them. Thus, his tutorage brought many people of his time to love him and know him. Through the knowledge and the beauty of his bearing with life, we became inspired as Christians. His true message to us all was that "*the door is always open.*" His philanthropic messages were easily understood through his virtuous intent and his welcoming arms into light.

As a great prophet of his time he was valued and loved by all who met him. He was a great healer and listener. Thus, despite all persecutions towards the end of his life, he gave unconditional love to all. Through his bravery and courage the Christian message is not about war, hatred, jealously, judgement and defiance. His message to us was about love of our one God and the divine message of Holy Angels. He was one Master of many and his love and respect extended to all religions. Through his belief in *God our Father*, he did not challenge and argue with his brethren. He welcomed all religions and belief into his lessons and did not decide who was right and who was wrong. His love extended to all. Through this message mankind can learn from him and other prophets about reasoning and love. The simplicity of this is to know that purity can withstand the challenges of darkness.

The mistakes of history must now be learnt and overcome with love, prosperity and change. Through the grace of God and his forgiveness to us all we can change and learn to accept, love and appreciate our brothers and sisters with life.

Jesus Christ taught us all that his belief was greater than life itself and from his precious life he gave us all his blood and life upon the Cross. He suffered for us all as humanity and the greatest gift of all was his love, kindness and courage. We as humanity have not as yet understood his sacrifice and virtue upon death. He gave us all hope and cherished the world at his feet. His forgiveness to us all is the very fruit of life and existence with God. From our world we have not as yet united in the belief of his gracious light. We as humanity must now learn and understand to follow his virtue with sanctity and love for a better future and world.

CHAPTER
FIFTY SIX

THE SOLAR BUTTERFLY

....

"Sunspots and butterflies equate to our understanding about solar change and the latitude of heat, telecommunications and atmosphere. The changes to our Earth through Eclipse, Sunspots and Equatorial latitude converge with the changes of magnetism to our Earth and her journey."

Elizabeth Jane Parker 2012

....

We *are moving into solar changes to our world* and her energies of light. The helium aspect of our Sun brings evolution into another phase with eternity. The questions and answers we bring are not about fear. God is eternal and through the quadrilateral aspect of geometrics and physics we learn about *Angels of Light.*

The Cosmic Alliance about our Universe is about seeing the reality of time and space but understanding the invisible power of light. The reality of our celestial body and life is to know we exist now. From this translation we can evolve our thinking and structures with life into one of positive energy and lateral thinking. We as humanity have taken from Earth and her resources but we can now change our thoughts into using the Sun with positive aspects of survival and our life by sharing with nature and her changes. We can utilize our hydrosphere and solar powers transforming our world into one of sharing and caring about each other.

The spherical practicalities with spin bring the energies of life into a new phase. The substantial reformation of God and life is about improvement. Through *Universal Strategy* and Cosmic Alliance we will all eventually transform our mind-set with realism and intelligence upon the Earth and her journey.

Successive generations will understand our unity and reformation procedures much more than we do today. Through equality and universal status with realism and light, the stories of today will seem a travesty with knowledge.

Emphasis will be upon sharing and caring about our Earth and her resources. Emphasis will be about God and light converging with nature and the miracle of life itself. For this is where we as human beings through history have not utilised our virtue, spiritual unity and respect of all belief and structure.

Thus, the Earth is changing upon her journey and our thought processes must be aligned with this. This is where we must all learn about the New Age of Enlightenment with Nirvana and our Earth herself.

Chi Chu Li – Buddhist Monk

The
Clock
Is ticking
Upon the wall
What measure of time it can recall
The ever turning of earth and hope
The love of god is eternal scope
Upon the sands of time it ticks
Upon the love of god emits
To cherish our
Lives for better or worse
Through channels of love
We reimburse
The heavenly chime of bells within
The heavenly blessings of god begin
To understand our lives with love
To understand the messages above
Are not about fear hatred or greed
But love and belief of god's creed
Those angels are divine and bring to us all
The gift of message to uplift and enthral
To never doubt the universal space
Living and giving eternal embrace
Our future sustains through belief and life
Not to doubt and cut like a knife
The Angels of God bring us our truth
Through divine science and life as a proof
Never to doubt the truth of being
Never to deface the reasoning of seeing
The beauty of life despite the mystery
Of learning and understanding

The mistakes of history
For god sees us all and is watching us grow
For life and reasoning is to always know
Through the channels of Heaven and Earth
Our connection with God and with birth
That Earth is eternal knowledge seeking with time
Learning, forgiving the messages refines
God loves us all whether we know
From Angels of love we live and bestow
Love and Honour
Humility and Challenge
Better for Good
Better for All

CHAPTER FIFTY SEVEN

THE EQUINOX OF CHANGE

....

"The hypersonic virtues of the great circle and geometrics of pulsar bring new beginnings in time. The Earth changes spherically and diametrically through space thus through heavenly connection and vibration evolution changes her being. We as humans have no power over this and thus our mind-set requires changing, The Spring Equinox and timescale identifies the alignment of hysteresis and isotropic formation with God."

Elizabeth Jane Parker 2012

....

The *accountability* of us all living within modern times accumulates our vision and aspirations with God. Through the emphasis of our Universal reality we must now all abide for the truth.

The retrograde aspect of *Reformation* is to understand the love and honour associated with God. Our God brings us all to understand the gracious love of the *Christlight*. Christ becomes us all individually, when we embrace the knowledge of learning with geometric timescale and belief. Our virtuous intentions with life become our strategy through believing in all of humanity overcoming the downfalls of dishonour and retribution.

Our lives are truly blessed by *Holy Communion* within our infrastructure and the global fellowship of God. Through belief our lives become truly blessed with Holy Covenants above the unreal aspect of delusional imagination. Through this understanding we can all find joy and happiness with the weaknesses of humanity and the aspirations of hope and integrity.

Through our world both spiritually and biologically lighting our path, we can address our weaknesses and downturns with love. Our pathway and journey with life is about learning and knowledge accumulated directing us all with *Holy Spirit* and gain for our here and now and future aspirations. We can all share and respect the humility and passage of our light. We can understand the pitfalls and gain our footings once again when we absolve ourselves and others through admitting and releasing the downturns. For our pathway in life always offer us a change with opportunity, and through the beauty of actually seeing and knowing about our journey with God, we can all proceed with dignity and virtue.

The teachings of Christ himself gave us all the beauty and love of the Holy Covenants. He illuminated his own path in order to demonstrate the truth and love of God, he sacrificed his life in order to present the door of actuality and benefits with love. There are many wonderful teachings from the past and they all unite within heavenly realms, for the mistakes of history have shown us all that we as yet have not united upon Earth.

The Kingdom of Heaven and Earth becomes us all through fellowship understanding our Unification and Light with Earth and her journey. God is about truth and blessings with honour. True love and the energies of immortal transformation into the realms of Holy Divinity and Angels Divine are about humility before honour. Our world will learn to change and in years of expanse with time, our fellowship will once more be at one. This may not be believed now, but through the avenues of time and space with Earth and her changes we will all begin to raise the vibrations of love, peace and honour.

Bishop Robert – Medieval Bishop

The Dawning

Elizabeth Jane Parker

The Robin sings his early songs
Proclaiming his position and where he belongs
The peaceful early morning light
The emphasis upon his love unite
He sings to us his beauty exists
And for an hour his melody persists
Encouraging the magic of early morn
The beginning of change is about to be born

Upon this Easter the beginning is nascent
The Earth and changes are not complacent
The quakes and seas of angry vibration
Is universal space and time with creation?
The major domino of plates and movement
Structure, foundation and celestial improvement
The magnetic aspect with time and space
We as humans can never deface

The Essence of time is precious to know
That we must respect and learn to grow
History and journey must comply
The Universal strategy we cannot deny
For realism and science is every day now
Our blessings with God is to avow
That we will be honourable and respect
Our future with God
Our future with love
Our future with change

Time and Virtual Reasoning

The *power and emphasis upon our lives is to know that everything we know today has grown from the past. Everything we own exists because of evolution and change. The photosynthesis with colour and energy through the light of the Sun brings our phrenology to hydrate with opposites both with physiology of oceanic components vaporizing through heat and sunlight into purity and hydrous composition. The chemical components of heat, light and vapour transform our world into a life force.*

The chemical reactions with daylight and night allow us all to understand the balance of monochromatic transition. The romantic and poetic translation of dew at dawn brings us to know a small element of beauty and spirit from the glistening moisture of natural ecology with life. The ages of life itself derive from fluid, light and air.

We are but a small element that has grown disproportionate through the ages of man. Now through the light of reasoning our planet must now reform and grow again in the beauty and wonder of The Universe. This small explanation allows us to listen to a dawning of a New Age with life and reasoning.

The very soul of our Planet is graced by the Universe and the powers of God. Our unification and understanding with life will again be born. We as humanity will reflect our souls of purity upon the Earth and her sphere.

Oh Holy Father and Mother of creation
Please sanctify and rectify all blessings of love
Bring our bearing and life force into renewal
Bless our planet of beauty and absolve the tyranny of the past
Bring us all into unity and love for God
Bring us to understand your ever changing pattern and journey
Bring us to love and honour you once more
Blessings are eternal knowledge.
Amen

Elizabeth Jane Parker

CHAPTER
FIFTY EIGHT

COLOUR CODING THROUGH SPACE

....

The Crystal clear elements of light bring us life and colour. From our monochromatic balances with mind, body and spirit we can all reform our truth and knowledge back into virtue. The trust of the Universe must be learnt. Only through ordination with God's blessings can we unite with the highest vibration. Purity must be apparent through truth, love, humility and honour to all things.

Elizabeth Jane Parker 2012

....

Through *the "echoes" of global catastrophe* our planet has transformed, reformed and changed again. Her status within the Universe is one of magnanimous colour, movement and life giving energies. Through her structure and foundation through eternity we have evolved through colour, light, fire, floods and great geographic upheavals.

Today is the 22nd May 2011. Our World is once more changing her plate movements and *xenon core* with particles, fire and disturbance. Mankind is just a speck of dust upon her foundations. How do we understand the *Heaven and Earth* connection with past realities and the relative calm of our modern lives? Ancient forebears' experienced massive eruptions and land movements. From this we know that through each millennium the waters and fires of time changed the Earth.

We as humans have overlooked our humility and fragility through this. We have no power physically regarding the Universe and the vibrations of time itself. We must all learn from this and understand that as individuals we are both humble and honourable through Angelic Assistance and "*Voices from Heaven.*" Our lives are given power through elements of chemistry, sustenance and oxygen. Our spiritual essence is formed through the evolution and eco systems of life itself. The misunderstanding and eruption of misrepresentation is now about the reality and truth of our Great Being within Heavenly Realms. We all belong this, however through the ages of man ego has evolved. Through self interest and phrenology misleading us all through lack of responsibility and belief, we as a world of one have become disorganised. This truth is very apparent today. This truth must now reform into virtue, honour, respect and love for all things of creation. Our world must now appreciate the gift of life and reasoning. Our world must now change spiritually and biologically into the realms of higher vibration and love for our Earth.

Responsibility is us all too know that Earth is a beautiful gift from God and our Creator. She is a magnificent aspect of evolution and life giving components. We must all understand our belief and creation through individual intelligence connecting with the virtuous reasoning of God and his Angels. This is not about fantasy but reality reforming and generating our *Planet of Life* for future generations to experience, respect, and honour and appreciation. Through our Angels and Cosmic energies our Earth will bring us all beauty, colour and light. Which in itself, we will gain a better concept and realities of our truth, honour, love and reasoning.

Native American Blessing

"Let us walk softly upon the Earth with all living things great and small, remembering as we go that one God kind and wise created all."

Famous Quote

"My soul can find no staircase to Heaven unless it is through Earth and her loveliness."

"Michelangelo"

The Opening

By Elizabeth Jane Parker

We Listen and see the break of dawn
The Blackbird feeds upon the lawn
The Sun is shining, the air with chill
We sit and wonder at the still
Of deviations that fill the eye
The laws of nature we can espy
Every day and in every way for us
We experience challenge unfolding with trust
We can lift our spirit with high vibration
And turnaround with elation
The miracle of youthful feelings

Transformation and soul, perpetually concealing
To know and learn about our lives
The one soul of light always thrives
With gift of sight
Absorbing our light
The symbol of physics and time
Allow birds into flight

The call of the Dove innocent and loud
His bearing and standing appears so proud
The Crow is humble and looks so dour
However into the tree he flies,
With aviation and power
Of speed and gusto into the branch
His being with nature is only to enhance
The placement of spirit so equal and divine
The knowledge of creation, evolution to define
That the garden will speak....
With the enigma of time

Knowledge is humble with the learning of senses
The treasures of God recompenses
The peace of the morning starting again
Every day we learn
Every day we see

Every day we can know
That we are in the service of God's
Words to bestow
That we are beings of learning invested
The journey of life is to be tested

To see the simple aspects of sight and persist
To know that we exist
To know that we are
To learn and prosper with beautiful thoughts
That prospective time unfolds and courts
From seeing creation
We are one with all things
That we belong to God
That we love......

The message of God is for us all to know
That virtue and reason will develop and grow
The century of change is about to begin
It starts with now from deep within
The birds will sing messages of trust
The eternal melody of their song entrust
The knowledge of time is to simply see
To know with Divine Love we can all be
Knowledge and proof that God loves the Earth
The beauty of life is not to rehearse
The next generation into a truth
Through mathematics and nature
We need no proof
Through the photosynthesis of light
We can all know God and reasoning...
His eternal might
To see
To smell
To feel
The Light of Being
To create the element of love and seeing

We must appreciate
In time, space and structure
In honour and grace...
Constructive lessons for the human race
Navigation and courage bring us all home
To know and follow, that we are not alone
With God by our side
And his Masters of fate
Through their teachings we open the gate

Of Heaven and Earth we have virtuous pride
The messages of this we must not hide
Be proud to know that God is us all
When we learn to follow his wonderful call

With the Earth and Heavens respite
That through the pearly gates we will unite
Our lives with virtue, peaceful and strong
And that the truth is where we belong
With God always

With Love and Heaven in tact
Home is where the hearts is, and that is the fact
Ownership, Nirvana and Earth as Heaven
For us all to know
The way home is the "place" to go
With mind-set
With body
With spirit

Blessings are eternal knowledge...forever

CHAPTER
FIFTY NINE

"The human heartbeat is the vibration of all connection within and without heavenly source. The micro particles of evolution have progressed through the voluminous magnitude of spin and retrograde direction. The essence of spiritual reformation is brought about by Angelic intervention with virtuous migration within the human sphere of actuality and learning. The expansion progress is the miracle of time."

Elizabeth Jane Parker 2012

Many *people would ask the question* as to why our *heart chakra* is the connective lifeline between Heaven and Earth. The consequence of this is to know that our heart is the rhythm of our Earth and her vitalization with life and reasoning. Through the elemental components and velocity moving through the *yang* union of movement and change, her ultrasonics of migration through space transcends simultaneously with *yin*. The balance of nature is the cause and effect of multifarious geometric symbolism and endocrine lifeblood with the miracle of water, sustenance and nutrients of life giving components. How is the explanation considered to be spiritual? The mind-set of reasoning is through astrophysics and mathematical unification with energy. The microorganisms are the reality of our hydrodynamics and biological components with change gradually passing through a hidden veil of light. This light is caused organically with atoms, cells and colour permeating through our Chakra system with invisible attunement and balance and colouration.

The Earth provides our nutrients and substance and being available to us all. However, through not seeing the superstructure of minute details of our life and reasoning, we take for granted the explanations regarding our life and existence. Thus, through her transitions and changes with time and space we all live within our modern world through time travel from past transition. However, the magic and reasoning of this has become unreal to many sceptics for God and light. The scientific proof must be fact and through fact our modern world disputes the actuality of spirit and soul. The reasoning of God and our Mother is to know that *yin and yang* of existence is the necessary attribute of God's messages to us all. And despite scepticism and doubt, mankind has forgotten the teachings of the learning aspect of time and space. We are all continual seekers with light and reasoning. Our journey with life is about us all appreciating and formulating compassion for those less wise and less able to see *"The Mirror Actuality"* with life and God as one. The beauty and transformation of our heavenly one is to see the Earth and her challenges through the yin of our existence with God.

Through this teaching most will understand eventually that we are all equal with God and the journey of life and reasoning. The miracle of our heart is to know that every day we are blessed and even with angst we can release this through Angels and love. We can forgive and release the hypertension of grief, stress, dishonour and downfall in a modern world of turmoil and dishonour. We can all begin to believe, transform and understand that our journey through life is precious if we open our senses to the wonder and beauty of life through the sanctification of Holy Orders once more. We can all once again climb the stairway to heaven, through symbolic placement with reality and reasoning. Thus, this is the message we must send through our heart for our brethren and sisters in fellowship with love, honour and truth.

"Anger is an acid that can do more harm to the vessel in which it is stored, than anything on which it is poured."

Mark Twain – American Author

Famous Quote

"All knowledge has its origins in perceptions."

Leonardo da Vinci

CHAPTER SIXTY

PEACE

....

"But wisdom that is from above is first pure, then peaceable, gentle and easy to be understood, full of mercy and good fruits, without partiality, without hypocrisy. And the peace of righteousness is sown in peace of them that make peace."

James 5.

....

The *peace of the Earth becomes an issue* for all of mankind when he fails to honour and absolve his weaknesses. All human beings are given the *"windmill of opportunity."* Intelligence brings a challenge to our belief and intelligence involves many stances. However, belief is individual and through this we can all follow our journey with self-belief but love and honour our brethren and sisters with wisdom and respect. Our purpose in life is to learn from every moment time is given to us all. Experience and learning are the fruit of life and reasoning. The fruit will bear seed if digested with wisdom. The fruit of life will germinate and prosper with intelligence understanding self-belief and the peaceful waves of virtuous intention. This will be a complication for many who lose their path and devotion for spiritual unification with virtue. However, the simplicity of virtue will be complicated when ownership chooses not to "listen" to the pure messages of heavenly source, and thus the shadow aspect of bitterness and greed will manipulate the energies with ego and the blessings of change will *cause stagnation within the waters of love.*

"We all aspire to our individual belief and conformity. Often we do not question our understanding of life. We accept that this is what life dealt me and consequently we become helpless and blinded by the light of reasoning through misconception and shadow. Influence will often show us all a direction we feel uncomfortable with. Through this aspect, we may hold to this dissatisfaction for our lives and spiritually lose our footing. Influence may entice us and we believe what others show us without recognition to our inner sanctum and resolve. We accept others opinion as our own and thus, our individual truth will not illuminate. However, we must all learn that divine understanding is within us all. To actually find our belief in virtue will gradually bring our self-esteem and illumination with joy."

Robert Grosseteste Medieval Bishop

The modern age brings the belief that money accumulated, wealth and glory is the treasure of life and many feel envy or admiration for those with wealthy status. However, life is about us all understanding our self-worth and the peace and contentment of life begin at *"home"* and where the truth of individual life excels. Within each and every person is the beauty and illumination of truth, love and peace. This will illuminate with every lesson understood and learnt, illumination will grow and prosper with strength, courage, wisdom, compassion, love, honour and truth. Faith brings our one the key of heaven when we fulfil our purpose and successes through life. We create our mind-set to guide us through life while listening to our *Guardians in the Universe.*

Our world of wisdom is failing at this present time but as individuals we can change the world. The four corners of truth will bring us all into growth and our soul will experience change and structure with a peaceful foundation. Through the simple messages of love and light heaven will assist progression. The

Holy Laws, however, must be maintained with great learning and absolve, divine will, divine truth and divine and acceptance. The beauty of life is our journey with time, use this wisely and all will unfold with wonder.

"Foundation is the flower in bloom. The flower is to enjoy and prosper with self-belief. Self-belief is to cherish our being. Cherish our being with knowledge, experience, intelligence, hard work, rest and play. Self-belief overcomes disappointment through determination and courage. Thus, growth can emerge when acceptance and challenge are overcome. Compassion and love will bring strength of learning and through our challenge being learnt and understood and we can illuminate once more. Foundation and truth is a journey for our incarnation upon Earth. Our existence is part of the wonder and evolution of nature and the processes of change this brings. We learn to overcome the challenges of time and accumulate knowledge for our heavenly structure. Our soul incarnates to learn and become supreme benefit for our space with eternity. Our soul is the eternal seeker of peace and transition into the realms of beauty and light with God and Goddess of life."

Chi Chu Li – Buddhist Monk

Famous Quote

"Learning never exhausts the mind."

Leonardo da Vinci

CHAPTER SIXTY ONE

THE REFORMATION AND CHRIST

....

"The Science of our lives is ever changing with time. The evolution of spiritual and mathematical alignments with physics and physiology bring us to change in line with the Zodiac. Through science and actuality with nature and her changes we live and learn through cosmic structure and enforcement."

Elizabeth Jane Parker 2012

....

The *simplicity of our science with life* is to know that we exist through a mega structure of evolutionary timescale within and without our cosmic reality. The pull and push of gravitational phenomenon together with time zones of the geographical magnetic needle of the magneto of Earth and her velocity through time and space, brings us understanding of our placement and realities with time. We exist.

The discussion during our modern age about the realities with science and spirituality is one of sceptic liberty and *hocus pocus* analogy. Finding the balance behind reasoning with mathematical assimilations and the concept of spiritual enlightenment becomes one of dilemma. How can one theory disprove another? How can the changes of time and motion bring our findings into one accepted agenda? The intellectual aspect of this is to understand the magnitude of our planet and her quantum mechanics within the proselyte of conversion and the writings of modern and ancient philosophy through the cosmic energies of yesterday, converting into a modern language and explanation. How do we as intellectuals and intelligent beings bring one whole explanation of life into our discussions with science and the light of God's reasoning?

Our home Earth still causes an unknown quantity of deep time and Hadean aeon with timescale and research. From theory and revelation the expansion of the Universe is purely speculative. Or is it? The same must be analysed about the human mind-set and the quantum mind and quantum theory. Scientists attempt to disprove the spiritual aspect of human thought processes and "out of body" experiences. Why do they need to answer this with fact and not truth? What is truth and what is fact? Questions and answers collaborate with each other through investigation and solution. However, the belief in sceptics is often preferable reasoning and against the modern idea of God. Again, intellectually we ask why?

The scholastic reasoning of every human being is to be challenged and therefore, with divining and belief about things we cannot see our intelligence can bring the knowledge of God and learning into each and every spherical motion of our daily lives. Through the changes and evaluation of cosmic energies with life and reasoning we can bring our hope and aspirations into divine discernment and belief. This energy is very real when we learn to understand our basic foundation with life. Through each and every thought we have is a miracle alone. This is not about loneliness, this about understanding individualism and forethought. Through understanding and procreating each and every day of our life, we can then feel Earth and her vibrations with that of our own individual stance. To learn and understand our wonderful Earth and her journey through space, we can all treasure and learn to love one another despite opinion and dishonour. We can learn to express our life with virtue but to speak with truth and love.

Despite Science and research, Scientists are the same as us all. They are fragile human beings with an enquiring mind into the fascination of science and reasoning. In this perspective we also question why as a fragile being do they attempt to disprove the wonder and existence of virtue and God? Faith throughout our world has brought many people strength and reasoning through their consciousness. Through bodily and physical disablement, they have secured their lives with belief and God's love and devotion. As with the Earth, there many unknown Epigenetic characteristics within DNA, and through biosphere it is believed in some theories that the bacteria from bombardment of asteroids, that human kind may have evolved. Again, this is theory regarding organisms evolving from deep within the Earth. Again, many scientists have different theories and through research they have diverted from each other concerning the truth and fact of science.

Even with this learning, mankind has so many questions to be answered through each and every timescale allotted with Earth. We know about the Earth and her rotation and orbit around the Sun. This again, is a miracle of our lives and truth. For this knowledge again, brings us all to "take for granted" the wonder of our Universe and the gift of life we all experience. For time itself has brought us into a modern era of sceptics and denial regarding the science of love and the science of fact.

As with the lessons from Christ and the timescale of our lives we move forward and understand that our challenges are learning, love and truth personified within our soul and the Earth. She is our mother of all things during life. She is our very reason to learn and appreciate life and our spiritual journey. So, from this first lesson we understand that we cannot disprove God and we cannot disprove science. From this lesson, we learn to understand the great prophets of our past. They did not have modern equipment and computers to research and disprove the existence of God. They had great learning and mind-set to absorb and teach all others the knowledge of the Universe. The miracle of wisdom was not analogised with powerful technology but through the Earth and her mystical journey within the Universe.

Despite the denial of many regarding God and his ministry, he is the good of all things beautiful and kind and thus to understand ourselves moving forward we all learn to appreciate his love for us all.

Virtue the Gift to Us All

"And now I come unto thee, and these things I speak to the world, and that they may have joy filled in them."
St. John 17

And *the Lord came to teach us all about the love and light of heavenly blessings and the word of God and reasoning. The love of Christ and heaven about us all understands our light with God. From our path and virtue with humanity we learn about our truth with life and the heavenly blessings of fellowship. Through our virtue we learn to understand our righteous clarity with sight. Through our sight we can learn to see "the light of humanity" an Angel's Degree within* *heavenly realms of love. Reasoning our love is the beginning of our life every day we embrace our understanding with forgiveness, light and God our father. Through the Yin and Yang of existence we learn about balance. Balance is about the differences of virtue accumulating with love and light. Love and light is about understanding the Earth and her gifts to us all.*

Elizabeth Jane Parker 2011

THE 'S' WORD FOR SCIENCE & DIVINITY 'SYSTEMATIC SYPOSIUM'

Part Six

Introduction

Elizabeth Jane Parker 2012

With *our true connection* with reality and reasoning we can all learn to understand our emotions and read their messages to us all! The messages of life and learning may encounter self-pity and unresolved lessons without objectivity and purpose. Our feet upon the Earth will feel all connection with heavenly vibration when we have truly cleansed and resolved our karmic passage with forgiveness and love.

The colouration and circumstance of our reasoning will indeed be a tough *thorn to extract* with reasoning our light against ill intent from our brothers and sisters. However, individual burdens cannot be released until mankind understands a purpose with forgiveness and absolve. Releasing deep injury from the thorns of adversity must be absolved with recognition and realisation. The Dark energies seek to invigorate ego with denial, and through denial darkness will absorb light with emotive resurgence and memory with reaction. Reaction with anger is the dark intent with dishonour and despite the wrongdoing from others, will mirror their anger with ownership. This will then distort vision with life and placement with *"continual baggage and burden"* it will then take our lives into another sphere of actuality and wisdom will be curtailed with vehement self-vengeances. Thus, denial and anger culminate our spirit with weight and unhappy consequences to the soul incarnate. Our physical materials will gradually assimilate physiological and physical disadvantages to our focus and actuality with the journey life and meaning. Thus, to release the challenge of burden with forgiveness and understanding is the seventh lesson of virtue. Before our soul can convert all knowledge and karmic blessings into Heaven's Gate, forgiveness must be apparent at all times of dishonour and disagreement. From this lesson with God and Angels we can then abide with time and measure showing us how and why we use our purpose with passage and knowledge combining all severance with ego from past mistakes.

Our emotions with life are to learn and prosper when we learn to utilize the sanctification of pure energies with angels. To visualise and transform disadvantage is about our self-belief with virtue superseding the challenges of dishonour and malcontent with our brethren and sisters of life. The magnitude of reasoning involves our journey with time understanding imperceptive mathematical energies of transference and the individual responsive responsibility we all have through our life and transference with time. This transference is impartial gratifications with atoms and chemical reactions.

The realms of virtue are indeed the purpose of us all and through light, sustenance accumulating bacteria and microorganisms' into a spectrum of change, our karmic transference brings gradual interception of pure energies utilising reality and reasoning with our brain functioning understanding thought processes with virtuous intentions and learnt wisdom through life's ups and downs.

The power of our individual universe eventually brings the parallel universe of instruction with light and projection of unseen particles into magnetism with gravity. Gravity attracts bio reactionary status and accumulation. The substructure and reformation with cellular growth causes a miracle of directives and messages with DNA and our imperceptive timescale. Our parallel universe then uses all positive and virtuous energies with biological transformation. All colour and light with connection brings reactive electrodynamics conforming to structure and foundation. Angelic microstructure with magnitude unfolds through us all understanding our healing processes with forgiveness and reasoning our virtue. Only through the beauty and bonding with our messages of light can we all move forward with our Earth and understand our being with hers.

With virtuous cleansing and learning through life our journey will become one of attraction. This attraction is not about desire, money or greed, this attraction is about belief in the evolutionary aspects of change and the miracle of timescale changing and changing again. Through our virtuous transformation with dishonour and downfall we learn about our divine status. This status will eventually teach us from another dimension about our purpose and journey as an individual and the amalgamation of all energies of love, light and reasoning.

The metaphysics of our sight is to learn about the things we can see and cannot see. Our sight with life brings great messages to our soul when we believe in virtue and beauty. Virtue is about our new age absolving darkness with humanity and the avenues of dishonour. Through understanding the composition of all areas of growth, we can move our ever changing experiences into a mega structure of life's opportunities. Many opportunities present themselves with some areas of downfall. This brings our bearing to use our wisdom and intelligence to overcome the disadvantages of negative lure.

The miracle of creations is about learning and understanding our individual purpose and education with Earth and her own journey around the sun. Our universe is one of magnificent splendour. To understand the micro energies and our universal structure as one is the ever seeking ambition of our soul and life upon this planet.

The emphasis upon mega structure and learning is but a small contribution to our soul in major. The assets of learning through time and space accumulated bring us to incarnate with new perspectives and vitality. Through karmic transition and understanding our divinity we can all eventually prosper in heaven and upon our planet of life with virtue showing us the way. Our repose with life is to know our soul in major and to sooth our vibrations with listening and seeing the facets of change, and through change we can learn and absolve all misgivings our society throughout the world currently embraces with materialism. We all need to repackage our disadvantages with the power of self-belief and virtue as our leading light. Our systematic reasoning will bring our placement within the universe to revivify and maintain our structure and foundation with life and reasoning.

Thus, we end this lesson with one thought:

Listening to our individual vibration is simply about understanding the power of connection with all of life. Our biological life is one of energy and cellular transformation imperceptivity moving with time and space. Astrophysics together with metaphysics brings our individual status into learning and moving with time itself. This miracle is taken for granted in our modern world of technology and modern day comforts and through invention ever changing with technology we are all apt to forget about nature, sustainability and the very food we all eat. The imbalance throughout our world of intelligence has overlooked the messages of God and creation as one. Through imbalance our current world is about money and economy superseding the reasoning of millions of years growing and changing the spectrum of life. Our future is now bound with mankind understanding the true messages of God and reasoning within our time with reality. Reality is ever changing and through this message we all need to find our fascination with our Earth and her journey through space. We are all fragile and through our life we all need once more bring truth and love back to humanity and our journey with spiritual unification.

CHAPTER SIXTY TWO

EARTH, LOVE AND LIFE

....

Our Earth spans 4.5 billion (4,500,000,000) years

....

The *quantum mechanics* of our very existence have formed, formed and formed again. With our modern day intelligence how do we understand the workings of our creator and that of The Universe?" How have we as mankind misunderstood our micro originations and that of our infinite Universe with the *knowledge of Science?*

Cosmic energy and existence is the continual infinity with research and reasoning. However, the wonder of Earth is often overlooked as a special and beautiful planet. However, despite the aspect of life and reasoning we overlook this. Our planet is indeed a gift from the heavens through the very miracle of existence and life itself.

The mysteries and unknown aspects of our galaxy and beyond are given scientific priority. And through this mystery we fail to actually see our home and her assets. Through the history of mankind, greed, money and status have become the desire of spirit and life. Through the history of mankind death, tyranny and authoritarian viewpoints have dictated life on Earth. However, time is limited through eternity for the fragility of biological existence. And through the journey with life itself the opinions and intelligence of mankind has currently overlooked the spiritual assignation with our world.

Jesus Christ came to teach us all about philosophy, knowledge and love. His reasoning was pure and graceful. His honour was without bounds. His love created a story of hope and belief about our *Father in Heaven*. However, through his beauty and reasoning he was damned, tortured and murdered. However, from this, the power of his love and belief transcended through 2000 years. His love and grace with forgiveness for brethren who "exampled" his knowledge with ridicule, came to shine a light for humanity. Through this, mankind's intelligence have again evolved and we live within a modern world of riots, hatred, greed and power. Through this passing of time man is still disorganised. The power of scientific reasoning has not resolved modern day angst, belief and love with God. Materialism, desire and opinion have brought us as one whole unit into disrepair. Why?

Science and belief are actually about the wonder of the Universe, life and meaning. Together they form a truth. Together they are about life and reasoning. Through the wonders of science we can use our knowledge and imagination to grow, learn and formulate a better world in the future. Spirituality although not seen, is about what is seen and what is not. Spiritually in the purest and most virtuous form is about God.

Chi Chu Li

Divinity is about science and life existing within a beautiful sphere and magnitude. Through unique transformation of our planet at this current time, we can once again appreciate each other and accept the differences we feel. There is not one specific code of life, and making sense of aeons is the impossible task of intellect.

However, at present our Earth experiences rotation of 360 degrees per day. Through her path and journey our *Weather, Oceans, Earth Crust and Core* experience changes. Through this knowledge so do we! In this instance how do we use this momentum with power and access to life with our individual intelligence and that of our collective association with fellowship and humanity as one code?

What do we learn every day and what do we appreciate about the wonder of existence? The emphasis is upon knowing our bodily vehicle with respect and also using the natural world as exploration. Learning and seeking eternity's forbearance is our intelligence, belief and love of God. Seeking our own journey through life is to know and believe in good. Despite the challenges beset us all we can believe in hope and credence. Despite the dilemma that Science teaches us, we can know that our journey is indeed blessed from an unseen truth and source of love.

To live with knowledge and reasoning brings us to appreciate that Scientists are also seeking and learning. However, through this they do not hold the answers for evolution and change with our Earth. For is she who teaches us with light and reasoning about the facts and truth of life and journey. Her journey through the Universe has brought to us 4.5 Billion years of transition and change. Through this epistemology with science and growth with spirit we can all appreciate our lives we can appreciate the gift of life. *The Native Americans* as one example of natural peoples knew and honoured our Earth. They only took what they needed and only grew with resources from her being. Through this, they lived contented lives. They appreciated both the science and spirit of reality. By balancing their vibrations with all living things, they understood about her very essence and vibration with life and spirit as one element. Through their ancient brethren and Holy Orders with God, they brought great wisdom.

Many natural people throughout the world today are diminishing. Again, we are losing a beautiful truth with life and study. Through a less complicated science, they lived with belief, love and truth for the contribution of all living things to their existence. From simple lives they enjoyed prosperity and spiritual respect for our Earth and her journey through the Cosmos.

"When we face our truth with virtue we will enable our understanding with progression and positivity. The strength of positive mind-set and virtue brings our purpose into alignment with Earth and her "moment of velocity" with Universal unification and all learning spheres. The placement of spirit with reality and reasoning will formulate and circulate with Earth's journey at exactly the right momentum and thus, brings our spirit as one with Heaven and Earth."

Elizabeth Jane Parker 2012

CHAPTER
SIXTY THREE

PSYCHICAL PSYCHOLOGY

....

Searching through life is the co-existence we have with our biology, thus to seek and learn gives us good health and vitality when we understand the humility of learning. From this our fascination with science and Para-psychology allows us to work as one element with Christ.

Elizabeth Jane Parker 2012

....

Belief *is the miracle* and motivation of every person and their timescale upon Earth. This lesson brings to us the reality and reasoning of virtuous intent. Our loves and lives with fellowship can indeed test our vigilance with virtue. Many people have not *seen the light* of love and virtue together. Searching for God and reason is the very foundation of our existence. The science and reasoning with cellular and biological mass is the testing and reasoning with God's journey through time.

The Golden Ratio of mathematics is not only about physical appearance and beauty. The mathematics of time is the ratio between the numbers of numerical successions with knowledge and purpose accumulating into *The Fibonacci* sequence, formulating into a flower of knowledge with life. Thus, we appreciate art and colour through the effects of this mathematical sequence. With regard to mapping our lives with the foundation square of strength, courage, wisdom and compassion the formation becomes the four colour theorem, from this we learn that the world has diversity, colour and meaning.

Through the simplistic explanations of mathematics we can learn to appreciate the infinite spectrum of galaxy formation. This is where the Chinese believe that the figure 8 is a symbolic notation of the Universe. Thus the, a, b, c, of reasoning brings our intelligence to realise the simplicity of beginnings, but the complication and expanse with infinite numbers of psychology, biology and material mass with systems biology and life. All of life has mystery and through this aspect of mathematics, from geology and physics we learn to appreciate the wonder of all things and creation. Fascination and intrigue give us all the tools to work with each other and appreciate the great diversions in research. This is so, with our soul. We continually seek to learn and find answers for the mysteries through life. There is no one person with the brain capacity to absorb all of the secrets of life and reasoning thus, our journey with each other and individually brings us wonder and research through our connection with *bioenergernetics, receptors, chemosynthesis* formulating with *photosynthesis* from light rays from our Sun. From the accumulation and attribute from hydrodynamics our body can transform and absorb intelligence and energy with God. Eternity speaks to every generation that lives and learns. Through learning and acceptance we find aspirations for our own individual path. However, we ask "how did evolution and time invent this phenomenon?" Through the imperceptible dynamics with change our lives have been brought to this time.

Through the above analogy how do we acknowledge and

seek with divinity by our side? Through the light reasoning our many diversions through life bring us to understand the workings of reason. This science within and without our incarnation is to know that we are not alone with God. Through knowledge and life, we seek forever and the allegory of symbolic message to us all. For many, scientific reasoning has evolved with Para-Science and Psychology. Through this explanation we can move into another sphere of learning. Through this knowledge we can all learn to appreciate individual experience with that of all people. Through this acknowledgement we can learn to respect honour and love our brethren knowing that we all share but have different paths to follow with our Earth.

Our imagination and life force is about the miracle within and without our Universe. From this simple explanation we can begin to realise the wonder and miracle of time, biology and *evo devo*. Our journey through time is the realism of spiritual journey with the dynamics of bodily realism. We can theorize this analogy with the knowledge that God truly exists within us all through the concept of imperceptible time and formation with matter. Our lives are real but we pass through life as if through a dream, for yesterday has gone and we move forward with our Earth and her journey. As has spoken before, we move ever forward with time and all aspects of yesterday must be lessons understood and lessons to be learned through our realities and thoughts within the here and now of revelation.

Humanity has many roads to follow but in our modern world we have not understood our intelligence as one species for the good of all things in life. Thus, our new millennia will teach us all to reform, review and reckon our integral calculus with life and spiritual journey.

CHAPTER
SIXTY FOUR

M THEORY – MYSTIC OR MAGNETO HYDRODYNAMICS

....

"The wise speak because they have something to say, fools speak because they have to say something"

Plato 428BC – 348BC

....

The *mystery of our lives is an introduction from birth with learning and understanding the wonders of life and meaning.* The contributing factor for us all within our modern age is that many inventions and comforts bring our life into an unrealistic *"time warp"* with knowledge. To bring about understanding and intelligence the resonance of our species has in reality *"come to a halt."* This may seem unacceptable with current day research but by the simple reasoning of modern day convenience, progressive intellect has now been *eclipsed* through monetary status and availability. The ideology of this concept becomes one of an *intellectual bypass* with perception, knowledge and objectivity through fact. The Science of reality is now during our modern age to pursue facts, monetary backing, scepticism and denial. The door has closed upon us all finding the truth and love of our Universe through this concept.

From simple explanations for complicated formations, we

bring about a growth for our electricity with magnetism causing +e and −e (*darkness and light*) contributing towards the *Fibonacci* sequence of knowledge and life. The petals of our flower increase from a, b, c with electromagnetic theory regarding the visible spectrum and the invisible spectrum containing orange, yellow, green, blue, indigo and violet. From this we know that the *white light* for which we normally encounter is a blend of all colours in the visible spectrum and the invisible spectrum of visual concept. During scientific investigation it was observed that from the development of the *quantum theory* that light waves were capable of *kicking* electrons out of solid particles called photons. The physics and revelation of our species is one of attraction and deflection of interaction unseen to the naked eye. From this research we can now understand the miracle of our Universe with colour and light formation with the healing aspect of radiation and kinetic energy with thermodynamics from Angels. The geometrics with the *Fibonacci* sequence together with the laws of physics produce and inflorescence with our Universe through the elements of purity, knowledge, forbearance and acceptance combining energy conservation laws, which infuse us all with heat capacity for our bodily movements and biological components with life. Understanding virtue is the divine science of reasoning with God. Disproving this analogy is brought through modern learning with science as fact but from this we move into the spherical motions of time itself producing this *en masse* with truth beginning to evolve with divine science and that of scepticism being dissipated through unseen photons from another realm.

Science and spirituality converge with energy during our lifetimes. We as human beings at this moment in time fail to appreciate our very existence through truth and fact with intelligence. Our connection with life is fundamental for our spiritual light and convergence with our soul seeking attributes with life itself. Through explanations about spirit and science we can all acknowledge the reality and reasoning of the white light. Our very existence is about colour and light transferring our energies into balance and equilibrium. From this we can recognize that we are all gifted and loved by God through the very miracle of *Divine Science* and motivation from our Universe.

We are warm blooded and a species of incredible potential utilising our knowledge with that of reality and reasoning our impermanence but to seek the ever changing aspect of our being. The fascination of history and modern theory is about knowledge combing the theory and revelation of our Universe. As yet, this has been taken over with materialism, denial and greed. As yet, we have to learn about *phase transitions* with time. The science of our light is very real and our connection with other dimensions is yet unknown to Scientists. Thus, divinity will continue to elude reasoning until we all understand the breath and beauty of learning, appreciation and acknowledgement of all brethren and sisters with life and reasoning.

Our Earth is the treasure of our Universe. Throughout each galaxy and millennia we live with unseen and unknown signals and codes for life. Infinity calls to us all. Thus, through the beautiful and mysterious planet called Earth we can journey with life and immortality. This is seemingly mysterious to us all about God our creator. But from humility and learning we can all enjoy the wonder and creation of time itself and the past history of formation.

Thus, with Plato and his historic philosophies we can learn that debate and research through science and intellect with divine discernment can bring a whole new aspect of our world with sustaining and believing in God and wisdom as one. The good of all things are true and honest. The trust of the Universe is about all combining our diversity with wonder, respect and without opinion. Through denial many people lose their way in life and thus to bring hope and science as one element is the strategy of God and his teachers.

Fundamental Reasoning & Electromotive Dynamics & Earth

By Elizabeth Jane Parker 2012

The *electromotive dynamics and speech* of humanity is to communicate our virtues learnt and understood with electrolytes and biology formation conforming to our natural electrocardiograph with life and time. Explaining the truth of our existence as humanity is to know the reasoning and blessings of virtue understanding our path with God. The reality of God and Science has yet to be extolled with virtue practising, observing and believing fact with truth.

Obviously the diversity and complications of individualism moving each day of life actually seeing and believing our escapement with Earth becomes a complication of nationality, religion, politics, language, interests and devotion to personal needs and desires. From this complication how do we all believe and understand the realities of *Universal Strategy* and the lessons of individualism with mutability. The realism of our Earth moving around the Sun has become acceptable knowledge through education and curriculum. The question here is *do we realise the miracle and wonder of our Universe with life itself?* How do we all begin to become fascinated with the concept of our association with creation and our Creator God our Father? How do we find and seek the answers of an awakening with reality and the unseen dimensions? Our Earth moves around the sun without average journey. Her movement and electrodynamics with space is not a perfect circle. She spins at approximately 67,000 miles per hour every micro second upon her axis conducting energy, vibration and hydrodynamics with life.

The reality of everyday life within a modern world of modern technology creating communication across the world is in reality connected with votary blessings of *God and his Holy Angels* channelling the reality of the Heavens. Do we believe this? Satellites, Rockets, telecommunications, computers, downloading, uploading and television are a reality for us to enjoy. So, in the light of reasoning as modern day receivers of invention how can we progress the realities of *God and his Holy Angels* with a world currently experiencing natural changes with vibration, electrodynamics and spiritual evolution? Through modernistic inventions and technology how do we portray predicate messages to us all through God? How as biology and realism can we all unite eventually together and live with vibrations creating on Earth a heavenly domain? Can this idealism become a reality through God and Science together? How can trust, truth and fact become one of powerful understanding and knowledge between rivals with belief?

Scientifically, we are today moving at this very moment

around the Cosmos. However, we have been created not with computers, telecommunication and general technology through mankind. We are a product of vibrant volatization from hydrosphere's co-ordination with objective electromotive vibration culminating with time and matter decisively coercing molecules, chemistry and the virtuoso of God's direction with life and Heaven as one. Through this simple explanation we all exist today. So, the question is how can we as modern thinkers believe, understand and procreate our everyday lives with love, honour and truth with knowing about God and our journey through space?

The answers and questions through each individual life is one of honour, creditability and truth. Despite the differences with belief and communication our votary communication with God is real and when we learn to understand the principals and journey with life and virtue, we can relate personally to *God our Father* and feel his vibration with us all individually with virtue. However, modernistically, virtue is not preferable and does in reality compete with modern technology overriding the beauty and truth with Earth and her connections with God. We as humanity need to SEE our Earth, each other and all that creation has provided for us to enjoy through life. We as humanity need to progress upon the *Wheel of Life* with compassion for each other and the future mysteriously before us teaching the values of virtue and the gold of understanding God.

CHAPTER
SIXTY FIVE

THE HYDROLOGY OF HYDROPATH

....

Where would we all be without pure and simple hydrodynamics?
Where would we all be without energy and sustenance?
How do we acknowledge and recognize this with existence and life?

Elizabeth Jane Parker 2012

....

Science *and divinity can walk along the shores of life* together as a wondrous formation and lifeline for the future and sustainability of our planet. Mankind has now evolved *out of proportion* with intelligence. Belief and proof are at *loggerheads* regarding truth and fact with revelation. Scepticism causes our *World as One* to imbalance the degree of wisdom. Mankind has learnt about greed, desire and immobility with light. Thus, the inception of our regular lives becomes one of *catabolism with reality and reasoning our light through spiritual intellect and wisdom.* Instead of embracing the light of God, many people believe they know better as without proof divine science does not exist with God.

Through modern life people born into world of fascination and revelation become one of diachronic misconception through not listening or observing about the miracles that everyday life produces. The newest computer, I-pad and I-phone become their reality and reasoning. Without actually seeing the world and miracles of transformation with nature and the reasoning and enlightenment through life, they often become lost. From this revelation they simply refuse to acknowledge preservation, wisdom and knowledge for our future and that of our children.

Proof is everywhere concerning the research and revelation of divine science and that of illumination. To recognize and realize that the world has been born through hydrosphere and elements with the production of cosmic energies that is unseen to the naked eye. And from this, we move into spherical challenges with emotions, choices and our journey with both spirit and biology. The mind, body and spirit connection with life is about us understanding the decisions and choices we have, but to acknowledge our passage with love, honour and truth combining with our intelligence. Our intelligence is the directive for which we must all follow. Through this again, we know that we exist at this time. We know that we have comforts and pleasures through the skills and intelligence of man's evolution and thought processes with time. The wisdom of our philosophies within heavenly realms is about the Heaven and Earth connection with life and spirit as our guides.

We are all of God's children, and to deny this as having no proof and believing that creed does not apply to the enlightenment and passage with life, is the sadness of all. The wonder of God who sets us all upon our journey is about self-fortification with Angels and we can all apply our journey with the *light of humanity* showing us the wonder of existence with virtue.

Thus, ends our lesson today and we bring love and honour to all those people who seek the truth with the seven sacraments of virtue.

Summer's End

Elizabeth Jane Parker

Our summer ends with wind and rain
Intermittent Sun our hopes regain,
For wet and wind bring no respite
The elements forge the circle of light
We walk along the lake and shore
The landscape of beauty, we look and explore
Along the way brings geese, swans and birds
No driving rain or wet disturbs
The quintessential spirit to enjoy our surround
The slippery surfaces of pavements around,
Lake Windermere upon this season of end
Beginning every day with hope as our friend
Of life and meaning the web of knowledge
That our eyes and ears are searching to forage.

The picture window in our room
Presents a scene of beauty and bloom
The sailing boats upon the water
The essence of calm will never alter
The tranquil beauty of life and wonder
Despite the changes of elemental yonder
For cold winds may blow across the lake
But people continue to enjoy and make
The plans of the day bring them mystery
The memories of today becoming history

Early morning rain,
Brings a man for swim
Across the lake his day will begin
Despite the cold and mist, of early morn
The geese feast upon the lawn
The flight of "Jackdaws" skimming the sky
Seagulls flying ever so high,
This picture of life is fascination for all
The day unfolds with change to enthral
The meaning of life brings us this way
That life is the mystery and decision today
No amount of prediction can change with the wind
No amount of speculation can infringe
The feeling of freedom from Earth and her gift
To us all if we choose to gain and uplift

The images of life that meet the eye
From imagination and sight, we can rely
With tourists feeding the hungry birds
Laughter and happiness can be heard
Photographs taken for memories to come
Through a journey brings time unsung
For meeting our brethren from other shores
Anticipation of joy for all ensures
That in the future they will recall
That England's lakes are beauty for all
Every experience brings us to change
Time immortal our soul to arrange
The wonder of spirit and journey through life,
We bring our virtue balance and light
With humanity and exploration,

Of gifts we all bear
That our beauteous planet is for all to share
Despite our world of fury and hate
Through beautiful places we can all relate

Humanity is intelligence to change our world
Into harmony and peace unfurled
For in spiritual place made from God
To know our Lord, our feet unshod
With feeling our way with virtuous intent
From this advantage we can invent
Harmonious living for our future
With Love
With God
With faith

The mystical Phoenix arises through faith
The wonder of science presents, ecology debates
The flight of spiritual freedom relates
Signs from Heaven, our destiny waits
The marvel of evolution will always follow
The love of Christ his cup to swallow
The waters of time is the marvel of light
To wait for the reason we all unite
Humanity will gain to know the truth
The celestial reasoning of God
The celestial reasoning of love
The celestial reasoning of Nirvana

CHAPTER
SIXTY SIX

PSYCHIC OR IMAGINATION
WITH VIRTUE

....

The love of the Universe is simply about learning divine discernment and knowledge. From this we all embrace the teachings and love of God and his followers. From this we move ever forward with time. From this we live, learn and appreciate the Earth and her gifts to us all.

Elizabeth Jane Parker 2012

....

The *impalpable concept of time and space* often becomes one of prediction by many people who believe in gift of physic phenomena.

However, through the journey with *Holy Orders* the emphasis upon our lives is about *wisdom and choice* superseding the desire of greed and often manipulation with prediction. Of course, we all feel despair and consternation at some point during our lives, but through these we can utilize and understand our lessons with virtue. Virtue and imagination are about progressing towards our goal and seeking through life and the obstacles that often prevent us from moving ever forward in time. Many spiritual people within our world often become lost and lonely through misunderstanding the power of belief and virtue. This is where human error will occur and the objectivity of spiritual enlightenment will elude them. The power and necessity of virtuous reasoning is not about *"hocus pocus"* imagination and glory in self-interest. The aspect of God and the Universe as one law is about seeking and finding our enlightenment and nirvana with Earth and her essence. The power of love is about respect for all life and God's blessings to us all.

We as individuals cannot understand divine discernment without determination and virtuous will. Downfalls often blind people into an analogy *"why does it happen to me."* Through negative E- in the scientific spectrum of learning incarcerates their being with doubt. Thus, through not taking responsibility they will often blame others for their decisions with negative lure. The truth in life is about E+ balancing with E- bringing *The Fibonacci* sequence transferring energies of minus into monochromatic balance with virtue. From this formulation we understand from darkness and ill thought that we can motivate our mind-set into balancing the challenging energies of life. Responsibility and ownership are important for us all seeking and finding with our energies and motivation with life.

Masters and Mistresses of Destiny advises us all through life and wonder when we listen to their instructions and divine messages. We must all understand that we are equal and divine through humility and honour discerning the messages of love, light and reasoning for God and his *Holy Orders.* When practising and teaching about enlightenment we must give hope and structure with love and kindness. Heavenly love is about listening and assisting with self-healing through connection and reconnection within our mind, body and spirit with life and that of others with humility and virtue as one.

Our Lord Jesus Christ did not put himself above others when teaching about life, love and reasoning. His messages were about us all finding the beauty of light during the challenges and misconceptions often brought to us all through this modern age. He embraced all religions with respect and honour for his love of humanity and brought the messages of our *Father in Heaven*.

CHAPTER
SIXTY SEVEN

THE DESTINY AND DESTINATION OF DIVINE PROVIDENCE

....

"We are all seekers within the realms of life and reasoning with God. The equality and definitions of learning and teaching are often met with superiority. However, ownership and nirvana work as one with time and space reasoning our reality with life."

Elizabeth Jane Parker 2011

....

Our *Lord Jesus Christ* came to us all as a man of learning and teaching the ways of God with *Holy Spirit* as his guide. However, the son of God was indeed a man of great knowledge through his teachings with humanity. His passage with life was ordained from the heavens and from this he gave eternal love and prosperity to all who listened. His praises and virtue of humanity was about *"opening the door for all people who wished to learn and gain knowledge of virtuous reasoning with life."* He was a man of deep love and humble bearing for humanity. He was a man of great wisdom and intelligence.

We as humanity within our modern age of intellect have as yet, not understood the messages of God and his teachers. Great honour was bestowed by *Our Lord* to all religions of virtue and *Holy Divine*. For we all have choices with life and reasoning. From this, history has portrayed tyranny and influence from those who believe that they are the answer to the learning with life. This unfortunate betrayal of virtue has now integrated into Society as a whole and from this diversity brings misunderstandings and a failure to process the word and love of God.

We as humanity must understand that heaven abides for us all to learn with humility, honour and truth. For denial has become the portcullis against *Divinity* and truth being heard throughout our world at present. The word of God is not surrealistic purposeless analogy but is realism with love as the power of change. We as humanity have to understand the virtues of God and his realms of reality and reasoning the karmic weave of life. Through life we learn about our individual status and practicality. Through life we all learn about each other and value with equity our individual gifts and creativity with life and wonder. For we all need to open our eyes and see the reality and vocabulary of our Earth and her life giving attributes. Heaven upon Earth is there for us all. To open the door is about learning and understanding that the key to Heaven is us all through our creed and love of each other. Respect, honour, truth and love are the words we highlight for our lesson with forgiveness.

Religion and belief are about virtue, honour and love for our brethren and from this *Our Lord Jesus Christ* gave us all hope about honour and truth being at one together in life. We are all brothers and sisters of light. To disbelief this is yet another sin towards the messages from great teachers and philosophers ancient times.

The love of *God our Father* is available to us all when understand that *"knocking on the door of heaven"* can be achieved by changing our perspective and intelligence with faith. Our faith and reformation is based upon truth. This truth is about our sight with life and reasoning utilizing our imagination with virtue and converting our electrodynamism. The gift of healing our vibrations with life can be achieved with focus, interest and realism being the journey we all seek as souls of *Universal Strategy* and intention.

Understanding and Forgiveness

Elizabeth Jane Parker

May *life once more bring you peace and happiness? May your road once more be apparent? May the love of Christ once more bring disparity into repair? May the eternal love of God be felt with aspiration and hope?*

Our journey through life brings many ups and downs to encounter. We may feel as though the weight of burden is ever present and unshakable. However, once we understand about God's love and passage with divine understanding our repose can once more be achieved.

Forgiveness is the very foundation of our belief and discernment with God. To understand this is the very hardest of lessons we all undertake when our brethren cause dishonour. Through mirroring their anger with reaction we often carry this weight without recognition of our individual responsibility. Love is the greatest power of all downfalls and to understand this is to know that our challenges will be set free with love, honour and truth.

The love of God shines for us all with wisdom and forgiveness against the greatest of dishonour. Thus, our faith will open many doors of beauty and love once more.

- THE UNIVERSAL FORUM -
WITH REALISM & VIRTUE

....

Part Seven

....

The Flower of Hope

By

Elizabeth Jane Parker

"Life if the adventure, wisdom our journey, love the answer and truth is our path"

The flower of hope is the advantage of sight
Understanding virtue,
The meaning of light
From hidden mystery knowledge will flow
And virtuous reasoning our heart can go,
Each moment, each day we awaken at dawn
Our path of wonder can never be worn

Spiritual path is the way of hope
Blissful feelings we can all cope
When disadvantage,
Challenges with strife
The upside of this is love into life
The landscape diverse,
To go off our path
Wisdom and patience overcomes our wrath
The shift of Heaven will unite with our truth
Always the answer of love,
Gives us proof
The soul of our Mother Earth aspires to us all
Messages from Angels can never be small

We carry our truth with privilege and love

The flight of the Eagle,
The heavenly dove
The comfort of messages,
Knowledge from God
The feet of Angel has always been trod
Walk with life,
Fascination to follow
The journey of time,
The wings of a swallow
Across dangerous terrain,
High winds can blow
Their passage on Earth is always to know
From starlight and rivers they follow the way
Endangering them,
Sometimes to stray
The illumination of flight going with the Earth
They arrive home to England to give birth
Babes will learn from ancient to now
The Holy Spirit shows them how

Life's journey will always bring us home
Through our God we are not alone
We appreciate the glory of time
Teaching us reason and spirit to assign
With virtue and balance,
Our individual innovation
We learn gift from life,
God's creation

We all work with God and future assured,

From intelligence and wisdom,
Continuity explored
The way forward is,
Never look back
Contemplation with life,
we will never lack

The majority rule from *Heaven and Earth*
The flight of the Phoenix brings rebirth
The teachings of virtue with God's plan
The purpose of wonder, life and man

The truth of us all,
Is about change
The shift of vibration now explained
We walk together towards our light
The questions,
Answers love to ignite
With reasoning focus, love and appreciation
Never failing our God,
And humble vibration
We all stand strong and thus procure
That life is meaning not to endure
We work and pray for us to enthral
That being with God is not boring at all

We work with love, honour and truth
We work with Strength, Courage Wisdom and Compassion
We work for our ONE

Ownership Nirvana Earth

Introduction

Theoretical Macrocosm and the Magnetic
Microstructure of Life

The *beginning of theory* is the continual question and findings
Scientists throughout our world seek to divulge with fact. However,
the history and formation of time is quantum mechanics with the
"sostenuto sovereignty" of emerging change and colloidal
transformation. Thus, the evolutionary timescale and mathematics
become a metamorphic question about life, the cosmos and our
universal prospective with reality and reasoning. The simple truth and
fact of diversity with research is ever changing.

We as humanity have been a minor part of the proponent aspect of
our planetary alignment within our galaxy conjoining with major
astral identification with cosmic energies through space. Our
intelligence from both simple and complicated idealism with life and
beginnings is theoretically a mystery. The ever seeking facts about
science and spirituality becomes for mankind during the twenty-first
century, one of who is right and who is wrong.

For example the English language is a number of 26 letters of the
alphabet and from this our communication is diverse and vibrant. From
26 letters our languages create a voluminous diversity of the written
word. The magic of word brings us to learn with recreation and
knowledge for us all to communicate. Writing and explanation come
into a fascination for many people who read and learn, enjoy and create.

Exactly, how do we perceive learning, knowledge and
communication with our fellowship and love of life and journey? The

history of our world began from a "ball of fire" and journey around the sun itself. Research, theory and speculation from microorganisms bring our well-meaning research to find and evaluate the treasures of biological transformation and messages of ever changing diversity. From these examples we move into the reality and reasoning of belief. How does science and philosophy teach us about life and the history of humble beginnings with time, intelligence and formation?

Scientists and Universities are ever seeking and learning about our Earth and her miracle with life and evolution. Learning and seeking with individual life is the gift we fail to understand about God and virtue. Opinion has through man's history been both influence and tyranny. As with global leaders power is given to people from the masses with ego and self-interest. Scientists work with theory and speculation about exactly what they see as fact. From fact the truth is non-apparent through opinion. ABC and our chosen dialogue are not about one person and their opinion. We as humanity must understand the fascination of research. However, what we can see through the Universe and the mathematics of speculation is an ongoing opinion for many Scientists about our "unseen" world of virtue and knowledge for our macrocosm of circumstance with our ever changing world.

Theory and revelation is about our infinity with divinity circulating and evolving with instruction, understanding and procreation with virtue. Learning is eternal knowledge and the fact is verified by belief and strength with hope and charity for all of life and association. From this we journey both with the stars and the wonder of life upon Earth. Thus, the diversity and evolution of change brings us all to refresh and update our knowledge throughout time and space.

Elizabeth Jane Parker 2012

"Divine Science

is about intelligence with trigonometry and geometrics working with unsubstantiated timescale and evolution. To understand this concept is the workings of mind, body and spirit understanding virtue, wisdom and truth."

CHAPTER
SIXTY EIGHT

THE TRUTH, THE WORLD, US

....

The *truth and reasoning* of our individual Universe within space allows us all to wonder at the expanse, Galaxy Clusters, dark energies, dark matters and exactly how the Universe began. The emergence of this with orbital investigation and space probes has opened our eyes to the literal expanse of "unknown quantity." Investigation by scientists and exploration with study brings many theories to our intelligence. However, proceeding with our interest in the immense structure of our Universe and mathematical assimilation brings us the knowledge of current day theory.

From the above introduction, we continue our research to find answers about the beginnings of the *Universe and Cosmology*. The many theories bring us diversions and interest into the person who researches with theorization. From this we now have many theories regarding our own Planet and that of our immediate Universe. The questions and answers often predominates the reality of God's existence within the framework of modern day knowledge. From this beginning we will bring a new and abstract contribution towards the science of life on Earth and the cosmic transitions and velocity of powers, throughout the planetarium of wonder and existence for our eyes within the twenty-first Century.

Mankind has developed many forms of diversity and exploration for modern theory but we must all understand how the ancient peoples grew their crops and lived their lives through understanding the stars and the positions regarding the quantum mechanics of movement and change. Without clocks our ancestors were able to determine the weather and future predictions of their livelihood. Thus, from this, many monuments were built with great challenge and belief about the contribution of the universe for life and reason. To understand the geometrics and voices of reason is to know that we are indeed blessed with life and sustenance. Great space and connection is for us to learn and know with appreciation and thus, this new book will bring many revelations to mankind. Through the dimensions of time and space mankind has developed his intelligence. Through experiencing the journey of life and reason is to understand the greatness of our own Planet Earth. Her contribution towards our developing intelligence has been a wonderful revelation to behold. And as yet, we as mankind have not learnt this. During the past century we have grown and developed with materialism but from this we are now causing devastation to our Home. The wonder of this could be lost to our children and their future. The wonder of God and belief through virtuous reasoning is gradually shrinking and from this we are losing the greatness of beauty and our planet of gifts.

Scientists of our modern era choose to discredit spiritual enlightenment and the belief in all things good. Our planets, galaxies and universe are realistically an unknown quantity. However, through our vision with hope and creditability we will begin to change.

Famous Quote

"A wonderful fact to reflect upon, that every human being is constituted to be that profound secret and mystery to every other."

Charles Dickens (Author)
1812 - 1870

CHAPTER
SIXTY NINE

MYSTICAL INTERVENTION OR TRUTH

....

"Our world of love and intellectuality is gradually disappearing without recognition of truth, honour and compassion for fellowship among men. From this our ship of humanitarian reasoning is "lost at sea" without sight and senses towards a future of respect, intellect and wisdom of God's teachings."

Elizabeth Jane Parker

....

To *begin at the beginning* is to identify our reasoning and wisdom with life and journey. The wonder of existence for us all as humanity is to seek and learn about life. Yes, is it really that simple?

Understanding and working with our biological containment and that of spiritual entity is to know that we truly exist at this moment in time. Our eye opening transitions with life itself is often beset with indecisive face value evocation with fellowship and love. We overlook as a species throughout our world at present, to see, smell, hear and feel our vibrations with Earth and Heaven as one.

Mankind is often racially insular and unforgiving. From this truth our World is now during 2012 oblivious to truth and the equinoctial transition. How can this change our truth, reasoning and worldly message of love, honour and truth? Our confusion spiritually has become a sad indictment towards the *Holy Spirit* and true messages of God and his love. Money has now become our enemy with truth and reasoning. The World has been taught through *the ages of man* to value introspectively possessions and materialism against the love of fellowship and sharing our world with respect, honour and compassion.

The inspiration of us all is now depleting against spiritual unification and love. Throughout history the messages and love from heaven has been challenged with dishonour throughout life's enactment and mankind's greed for power and glory. Exactly how do we progress with this emplacement with life's journey and immortality? The truth is how do we as fellowships follow our Earth and her journey with understanding, love and compassion for all things created by God our father?

We all deserve to find love. We all deserve to be enlightened. We all deserve to find our love and compassion for our fellowship in life. So many people undermine the truth and validity of love and reasoning. We are all brothers and sisters throughout eternity and creation and from this we all need to understand our individuality and messages from God and his followers with true love and compassion.

Many people misunderstand and fail to see the beauty of spiritual path and biological journey. Our humanitarians' ship upon the *waters of time* often becomes disrespectful and elusive with the journey of light and message. We all fail to see each other and the connection we have with the *Universe and the Earth* as one element. Our connections have become blind! As a species of great intelligence and learning we must now all redeem our light with God and reasoning.

Guildford's Autumn

By Elizabeth Jane Parker

The love of God with sight and sound
Is a journey of experience so profound?
Biologic lamp of light and truth
The foundations of delectable proof
To use our mind and wisdom with sight
Upon the steps of heaven recite
That a passage of love and wonder perceive
The miracle of living we cannot deceive
Our association with life, and others conform
A daily practice we can perform
In using our senses, the purpose of filtration
And humility within our own vibration

The journey of life brings many to know
About our world to learn and grow
The basics of life brings us to see
And know our life with all to be
The future holds the secrets of time
We understand our destination and assign
The sights and sounds of living with Heaven
Through kindness and understanding with
Our brethren

A walk through Guildford's High Street today
Brings us the people in fine array

Of shopping and seeing varied faces
Integration and reasoning, our mind embraces
Clothes for sale in many shops
Windows displayed with expensive props
Colours and fashion to draw the eye
Expensive ranges for us to buy!
Into the bread shop to buy some lunch
Happily awaiting a time to munch
The delicious contents of baguettes and rolls
Planning our picnic to the park we stroll

Once we are sitting to see all around,
Enjoying the ambience of our surround
With people experiencing the beautiful day
Marigolds and flowers bring their display
The colours outstanding upon the beds
Within the park the leaves of autumn sheds
The delight of being together is free
There are places that we can all be
Without the meaning of money and gain
Within commercial towns, for people to remain

Workers from the office take time to enjoy
The pressures of work from their employ
Walking to the Castle, to view the scene
Of Guildford's beauty often unseen
From the perspective of history,
We stand in our place
From times that have gone from the human race
To stand at this moment upon ancient steps
We look and perceive change and aspects

That many years ago, would now be unknown
From evolution time has shown
The difference of our modern age
For us to envisage and hope to engage
With knowing that man has developed from this
Seeking the blessings we cannot miss
Because it is there for us all to explain
Modern day living with love to sustain
The freedom of spirit is about the event
Appreciating the smallest reason and advent
Our imagination with life, reasoning the spectrum
Mirroring our individual spiritual connection

The Cathedral stands so beauteous, upon the Hill
From war and peace was built to fill
The heavenly knowledge of God's truth and blessing
Faith and reason is indeed refreshing
The foundations built by purchasing a brick
The walls contained are now so thick
Patience through a war, to finish with gain
Upon the hill she will remain
For all to see with pride and glory
Built with patience, to tell a story
That faith is available within our time
A modern cathedral new to combine
The love of God is worth the wait
For this beautiful Cathedral, our love will make
The doors are open for all to see
Humanity and patience of divine entity

Building a spiritual love, determination and skill
The flight of the dove inspires our will
To live and learn, this place called living
Eternally respecting and wilfully giving
To maintain and preserve this wonderful attainment
That life will provide free entertainment
With virtue, with sight with honour
Into the arms of God
Into each day
Into our lives

Forever

Heaven sent is...

The love of God our father and creator of virtue with prayers of peace and love for all who listen. Our paths are a placement we all seek to follow and once more find peace with life and reasoning. The attributes of us all is to love, honour and obey the Holy Covenants of God. Love is us all when we truly understand our journey.

Twilight Excursion

Elizabeth Jane Parker

Softly, softly our footstep will tread
Through the elements of karmic thread
We follow the Earth with love respite
The dusk is shedding a grey dismal light
Our thoughts are about the wonder assign to thee
Waiting quietly for night to be…

From the above prose how do we as human beings appreciate and understand the formation of life with God?

Our *Starlight Innovation* is to wonder about the beginnings of time and the Universe. Our Earth and her mysteries remain today despite the theories and factual disposition of Scientists. As yet there is no definitive answer to our Universal beginnings. The night sky tells a story of Stars, beginnings, endings and infinity. The mathematics and geometrics of circular composition with our Stars is again one of a, b, c diametric formation based upon molecular density and gas. The centre of gravity and "Spectroscopic binaries" circulate around the cosmos with purpose and definition. From a Big Bang again we ask whether factual intelligence has created this knowledge. Why and where did our biology accrue intelligence and foresight with a fragile and complicated composition?

The question about intelligence is we ask Scientists again, how and when did our brain accumulate a quest and purpose with fascination and research? We know of our electromagnetic forces with biology and the miracle of this device. We know that somewhere along the processes of evolution we made dramatic changes to our physical and intelligence. We know that primitive to productive we have grown and changed our molecular geometry. From these examples we give a simple analogy with questioning. Yes, questioning!

Again, we move to Science and biology from their birth and lives with schooling and lessons they bring the wonders of the Universe with fact but they have yet to proof theory and revelation about our beginnings and teachings with intelligence as a basis of knowledge, foundation and the whole picture of life and meaning to humanity.

The question here is with so much opinion and knowledge throughout the world we have yet to fully appreciate the wonder, creation and amazing planet we live upon. Why, with so much around us and the minute particles of existence were we created. From whom and where did we form as a species of mystical, magical and a breathtaking creation with all of nature around us. Why do so many people believe in God as our Creator? Why do so many people have experiences and beauty bestowed? Why do we as God's creation deny him through fact?

Jesus Christ came to us all so many years ago. He came as the *Son of God* to show us all about our truth and intelligence with the Heavens upon Earth. He came to show us all about humility, honour, love and truth. His lessons to us all were about creation and the simple path of wonder in life. He came to explain and give to us as humanity the beauty and truth of the Heavens. He came to show us love. Love and intelligence about all things divine. So, from his teachings what as humanity of we learnt about truth? Truth is us all as one. Truth is infinity and definition about our spiritual and biological pathway upon Earth.

Love what is love? Love is about the wholesome aspect of humanity believing and seeing all of the good above the bad. Love is us all when we choose from our celestial intelligence among the facts and the science of the stars.

CHAPTER SEVENTY

CAST UPON THE WATERS OF TIME

....

"The transcript of reality is about culmination of knowledge with the waters of time and blessings superseding the imbalances of life's journey. Mankind has yet to grasp one droplet of conversion for our future with light and forgiveness."

Elizabeth Jane Parker January 2012

....

How *does mankind* as a whole actually culminate intelligence with Earth's journey with time? *The waters and mirroring* effect of us all is now undermined with diversity of opinion and fundamentalism defying the truth of God and our Universe. The mathematical assimilation balanced by the *Chaos theory* is discerning *determination* with the actuality of Universal Structure. However scientific forum is often dissimilated by Scientists investigation and the theory *"did the chicken become before the egg or vice versa?"* How did life begin? Many theories exist and are executed with fact and findings. However, one revelation to us all is that time changes life and evolutionary status. This knowledge is speculatively identifiable by research and the evidence of artefacts produced through the spectrum of space and reasoning. So, we ask about DNA and the building blocks of life. Where does the directive begin and end with intelligence and the formation of our planet?

Our Planet has lived and died with species changing and

new ones emerging. The aspect of this time changing development has caused speciation to climate and environment. The balances of this exist with creation emerging into a natural intelligence and spiritual unification with heredity. Biodiversity teaches us about terrain and the photosynthesis with light and plants providing food for many organisms. How does our modern day thought process evaluate the importance of balance?

The question of symbiosis and conservation of our Earth and her own natural development has now become at crisis point for humanity and the imbalances of infestation with magnitude. The threat is very real and yet we have not heard but seen the effects of deforestation, carbon fumes and air pollution are currently being absorbed into the atmosphere of the Planet. How do we take responsibility as human beings to the reality of this? From ignorance and greed the uncertainty of our future hangs in the balance. This is not fact, this is truth.

The process of us all is to demonstrate our individual forum with each other but to actuate our inner strength with divining our virtue with life. Is this easy? Darkness of over light is often preferable for us all when learning life's path. Darkness supersedes the monochromatic imbalances of impassive compassion and we as humanity make judgements on each other.

Science and spirituality are at loggerheads and the disrespectful truth about fact being the reasoning of our planet. In this, we ask the question where we are going as humanity with our current modern world into the future with fact. What exactly we do we all see in life? Can we identify our reasoning with God's will? Can we appreciate, acknowledge and preserve our status within spiritual path and learning. Can we know our truth accumulating with virtue? How do we see virtue? These questions are the very foundation of our lives with God, Earth and life. Do we believe this?

The World of Spiritual association with God has diversified into a melting pot of confusion for us all. Religion and faith has become litigious. Greed has been intrusive for us as fellowship and the knowledge of love is a place name of condemnation against respect and message from heaven. Preaching or teaching is about fellowship now ignoring important sonorous examples of learning and has become one of monotony. How do we grow and move forward with our Earth?

The love and truth of God is still believed for so many of us. No matter what religion or creed we belong to each other. We are all from the Earth's journey but as yet the fundamental sanction of love is a long journey to take. The blessings of life begin with us all understanding and teaching our children about their world and future with both God and our Earth. Until we all see this as universal the creation of dishonour will continue. From this knowledge we should all now gain understanding with our diversity but to know that we are the creation of time itself. From this knowledge we should all learn to appreciate and acknowledge our gifts and wonderful intelligence seeking time as biologic lamps of virtue.

Spring Time in Dorset

The evening has come, the rain as stopped
Continual downpour our day has been cropped
By misadventure our downturn has gone
Everyday living we learn to be strong
The turnings of life always to pursue
Yesterday's sorrow has now to renew
Waiting with time relaxing with peace
Stresses of life we can now release

We hear the thrilling beauty, of birds in song
The spiritual placement is to belong
The new day is here with peaceful quintessence
Our soul feels the union of tranquil essence
The new day brings the sun into light
Heaven and Earth can unite

Waiting together for our amiable friends
The early morning chill often descends
A trip in the car to a car parking place
We easily find an empty space
Dogs running happily along the beach
Carrying their toys, out of reach
Pushchairs and mothers, runners go by
The sky blue horizon to meet the eye

Walking to "Sandbanks" three miles at least
However the sights and sounds, our eyes can feast

Colourful beach huts different in design
Bear marks of the sea rusting decline
Wood boards with peeling paint needing repair
Our imagination causes us to stare
With wonder about, how small they appear
For families to stay throughout the year
Deckchairs for few to sit in the Sun
A holiday spirit although cold, has begun
Elderly folk amble along
Hand in hand they truly belong

The coastal sights and cliffs surrounds
With diversity and wonder abounds
Windsurfing the cold wind blows
Over the rolling waves their board goes
We walk together chatting out loud
The springtime of March, without the crowd
Building on "Sandbanks", more to be built
Some older houses cracking upon silt
Lizards protected within some tape
The natural environment taken to date
A token and gesture to preserve these creatures
A small place for them, token features

Six miles we walk in time for tea
At the Bowling Pavilion we wait and see
All the pleasure we have truly enjoyed
Making use of time employed
With every turn we see our light
Gone is sorrow into the night
Today the sun shines with a chill in the air

Walking with friends we stop and stare
At the beauty of Dorset our journey starts
Navigation and essence our spirit charts

Heaven speaks with one voice to us all
With sight of living we feel and recall
Life is the adventure for us all to share
Demonstrating containment for us all to care
Moving forward into the arms of God
Moving forward together
Moving with love, honour and truth
Moving with Strength, Courage,
Wisdom and Compassion
Moving with the tides of fate
Moving towards Heaven's Gate
With true love

Amen

"The reasoning ...

of our lives is to follow our virtue without false pride and revelation about God and truth. Through learning and understanding knowledge of the Heavens we all find love and the reality of life. Through our determination to follow a path of light with education brings us all to know the meaning of reality and reason with life and journey."

Afterword

"Focus and attention to life bring our perceptions into reality with the attributes of gift and sight with God. To understand the beauty and foundation of our Planet is about appreciation, thus we can move forward with sight and belief incepting absorption of bodily functioning with spiritual attainment."

The *sight of God* is us all understanding and appreciating our lives with virtue. Once we understand the virtue of *Heaven and Earth* as one, we as humanity can move together into a future of peace, containment and love.

From our association with each other we can bring forgiveness and love into our world of humanity and understand the freedom of our eternal spirit with life. We do not presume to know more than others within the sight of God and reasoning, but to bring equal discernment for all through compassion. We must find our reasoning with virtue superseding the darkness of desire judging and maligning our brethren and sisters of life. Through understanding with sympathy the darkness that has befallen them we can truly embrace them with love. To release our own energies of self-satisfaction we can bring our love to bear their fallen manner with God.

Our pathway with God is about seeking our divinity with honour and love opening the doors for all who wish to know and abide with life and reasoning. The challenges through life bring our learning and faith to bear the cross of suffering we can encounter with spirit and bodily unity.

The Messengers from God fill us all with joy and freedom when we truly listen to their messages about reasoning our lives with virtue. Thus with virtue we follow "the light" of God and the forbearance of Angelic Law. There are many lessons in life to both embrace and to know wisdom over adversity. For faith is the "footprint" of our Lord Jesus Christ when seeking the messages of divine discernment and love of all. Mankind has become during our modern age, a sad indication of darkness over light. His sight is set upon materialism and often self-interest. Thus, through avenue of karmic weave the threads will be cut and left without a needle to sew! Thus, many threads will be incomplete upon the pattern of virtue. Our Lord gave us hope so many ages ago. From his footprint and suffering his purity was a gift to us to know and seek his love. The Light of Christ is always available to mankind. However, the focus of life and being often confuse us when we lose our path. From this Heaven gives many gifts for man and woman to follow. From this, we can reason the gift of sight with our Earth and her beauty when we truly seek with faith and wonder. The teachings of Heaven are available to us all through the channel of light and virtue being at one with our physiology in life.

Our Biologic Lamp is the ship upon the ocean of life, through this analogy we understand our responsibility with virtuous reasoning. This is the wisdom of perception, listening, learning and knowing our purpose with life and God our Father. The reasons of our existence is about blessing those that are unfortunate through health, emotion and life's burdens with cruelty from our brothers and sisters who residence in darkness brings them great unhappiness. Despite the evil and corruption of darkness our lights and belief can bring God into the arena of life with reality and reasoning the journey with Earth.

311

To walk with God and reason is the life seeking aspect of us all. The Universal Strategy and our journey are about finding love through the maze of misunderstanding. Letting go of all burdens and disruptive mind-set and absolving the feelings of hate, mistrust and disruptive energies within our time and space with life. From this lesson many do not see, many do not know and many have lost their faith through life's battles. To encompass and embrace the path of enlightenment is about tomorrow finding and seeking our light with God and his Holy Angels. The journey we embark upon is about the reasoning of so many distractions and downfalls that life may bring.

But when we truly find God and his Angels with Earth, we can indeed bring Heaven into Earth with our vibrations of purity and understanding the light of our Lord Jesus Christ and the many teachers before us about wisdom and love from our Ancient Forbears.

The love of God is a powerful reason for living with our brethren of disrespect and ill-gotten knowledge. However, through many downfalls we can rise again into the light of reasoning our virtue with wisdom. For wisdom is the greatest gift of our spiritual communion with life.

God is the truth and beauty of our salvation with virtue and thus, through all avenues of humanity we can find hope within our modern world of confusion. Many have yet to find the path of beauty and wonder with understanding our fellowship and the aspect of all religions sharing Holy Communion with faith and belief shining the light of love upon our troubled world.

In the beginning…

"Was the word, and the word was with God, and the word was God. The same was in the beginning with God. All things were made by him, and without him that was not anything that was made. In him was life, and life was the light of men. And the light shineth in darkness, and the darkness comprehended not."

Spiritual Assignation with Robert Grosseteste Bishop of Lincoln to Elizabeth Jane Parker
June 2012.

From *this analogy how do we as humanity* acknowledge, feel and believe? Diversity and wonder are the eternal messages through life and reasoning. As individuals how do we all communicate, achieve and organise our thoughts in metaphor? How do we all believe without proof?

The love of God within modern societies is simply one of fragmentation and legend. Opinion and procrastination are often corporeal and corrosive towards the true love and meaning of divine word. Our Societies have now evolved with commemoration with money as a spiritual directive through life. How do these affect our natural world and the sustainability of a future existence with Earth? What actually are we all taught to understand with the miracle of life and journey?

The wonders of our Universe and the beauty of evolution and expansion with eternity give us time and motion with realities. The truth of this is we are all part of the most powerful energies and theism through time and space. We have yet as mankind to learn the values of this.

Our intelligences and faith are diverse and interesting and despite the evolution and lessons of war, greed and hate we still continue to disagree about the beauty, revelation and learning of life itself. The meaning of life is indeed fascinating and wonderful when we truly see and feel our planet of propinquity with time and space giving us all life.

Jesus Christ was one man who came to teach us from his learning with life and reasoning. He was one man who gave to us all with devotion and love within the realms of reality. Despite his messages of love and truth modern day peoples of the World follow a religion of digression and opinion. However, this religion is again fragmented through history with hate and diversion with the truth and messages from our Heavens. So, how do we go about change from a world in confusion? How do we as humanity formulate and change for a better world with Universal connection and true love? The ages of man have yet to connect and as one with *Heaven and Earth*. Virtue is the key to all living things with Heaven. Thus, our journey in life is the miracle that God gave us to follow.

Our modern world is a beautiful place and once we all see and learn this we can be at peace. Until those times yet to come as mankind, we will all travel the maze of life ever seeking and learning from Earth to find our One, Ownership, Nirvana and Earth.

May God bless you all with love, honour and truth.

www.ingramcontent.com/pod-product-compliance
Lightning Source LLC
Chambersburg PA
CBHW051940090426
42741CB00008B/1215